DESIGNS FOR CHURCH OFFICER TRAINING

HESTER M. ALLEN
PAUL W. ALLEN

Discipleship Ministry Team
Ministry Council
Cumberland Presbyterian Church

February 2014

8207 Traditional Place
Cordova (Memphis), Tennessee 38016

The Discipleship Ministry Team of the Ministry Council of the Cumberland Presbyterian Church is the successor organization to the Board of Christian Education of the Cumberland Presbyterian Church.

Funded, in part, by your contributions to Our United Outreach.

Originally published in 1989 for the Cumberland Presbyterian Churches Federated Board of Christian Education by Frontier Press.

First Edition 1989
Second Edition 2014

Published by The Discipleship Ministry Team, CPC
Memphis, Tennessee

ISBN-13: 978-0615979595
ISBN-10: 0615979599

OUR UNITED OUTREACH
Made Possible In Part By Your Tithe To Our United Outreach

Table of Contents

* These designs are suggested for pre-ordination training.

Introduction

Designs for Church Officer Training is a resource for persons responsible for the pre-ordination and continued training of church officers (elders and deacons). Some designs may also be adapted for use by church committees and officers of various church organizations such as women's and men's groups.

The topics for the designs were selected on the basis of needs expressed by persons responsible for leadership training and data from a questionnaire circulated by the Federated Board of Christian Education to representative pastors, elders and deacons in presbyteries of the Cumberland Presbyterian Church and Second Cumberland Presbyterian Church.

The Confession of Faith and Government of the Cumberland Presbyterian Church and Second Cumberland Presbyterian Church is used as a basis for content of the topics. Each design includes specific directions for implementation. The designs can be used as a series, each building upon the preceding one, or used independently.

The study material may be used by pastors or skilled lay persons in training, members of church sessions and/or diaconates or by trained consultants recruited by a congregation to conduct officer training. It may be used in churches with small or large membership and in retreats or other settings for leadership training.

Time requirements are estimated and will vary according to the size and experience of groups. Large groups will probably require more time for the activities.

Duties of Elders and Deacons

Focus

The church's *Constitution* (Article 2.74) states that persons who accept the responsibilities of the offices of elder or deacon should engage in a study which will prepare them for these offices and that they should continue to study during their tenure as church officers in order to better perform their duties. This training will assist participants in identifying and interpreting the specific qualifications and duties of church officers as outlined in *The Confession of Faith* and *Constitution.*

Time Requirement: 2 to 2½ hours

Objectives

At the end of this study, participants will be able to:
1. define and describe what it means to be called to serve as a church officer;
2. identify and interpret specific qualifications and duties as outlined in *The Confession of Faith* and *Constitution;*
3. list present priorities in relation to those duties;
4. express personal goals for performing their duties;
5. identify resources to assist in fulfilling goals.

Preparation

1. Gather resources: Bibles, copies of *The Confession of Faith.*
2. Obtain supplies: felt-tip marker pens, 5x7-inch index cards, masking tape, paper and pencils, newsprint sheets.
3. Print objectives on large newsprint sheet.
4. Duplicate resource sheets A-1 (Plans for Fulfilling the Duties of My Office—Elder) and A-2 (Plans for Fulfilling the Duties of My Office—Deacon).

Procedure

INTRODUCTION

Many church sessions and diaconates become "new" each year because of the rotation of elders and deacons. In order for participants to be at ease with each other during the study, a few minutes should be spent in getting better acquainted. This activity is especially important if the design is being used in a retreat or workshop involving officers from more than one church.

Activity

Using a felt-tip marking pen, each person should prepare a name tag by folding a 5x7-inch index card in half, printing his/her name on one side and placing the card upright on the table with the name visible to the group and leader. The participants then introduce themselves, identifying their church office and also naming two other roles (such as mother, teacher, engineer, nurse, retiree, et cetera) by which they are known. (about 5 minutes)

BEING CALLED TO SERVE

Becoming a church officer is an experience which may be interpreted in a variety of ways by those elected. There are also some individuals who may have accepted office without a clear understanding of what it means to be an elder or deacon. The following activity gives opportunity to explore personally the meaning of being called to be a church officer.

Activity

Distribute paper and pencils. Ask each participant to complete the following statements:
1. When I was asked to become an elder or deacon, I felt _____
2. I understand being called to serve as meaning _____
(5 minutes)

Ask several participants to read their statements. Give others an opportunity to voluntarily read theirs. Encourage discussion of the second statement by asking such questions as
1. How is being "called" more than just being nominated and elected?
2. How is the "calling" different from that of any other Christian's calling?
3. How is it different from the "call" of the ordained minister?

IDENTIFYING QUALIFICATIONS AND DUTIES

The *Confession of Faith* states that "Jesus Christ as Lord and head of the church has entrusted the government of the church to officers who make those decisions that will guide the life and ministry of the covenant community" (Section 5.32).

The origins of the office of elder reach back into the history of Israel in the Old Testament, specifically Exodus 3:16, 18:24-25, and Numbers 11:16. New Testament references relating to the office of elder are footnoted in the *Confession of Faith* (Sections 5:32 and 5:33 on Church Government).

The office of deacon is rooted in the New Testament. Acts 6 tells of persons being chosen for special responsibilities in the early church. I Timothy 3:8-13 gives qualifications for deacons.

Activity

With the participants working in pairs, ask each pair to use the *Confession of Faith* to read the references relating to elders and deacons (noted above). Ask each pair to discuss the scripture passages, identifying the qualifications mentioned and the duties named or implied. (15 minutes)

Reassemble the group and continue the discussion with a spokesperson from each pair contributing ideas from their study. (10 minutes)

Alternative ways to conduct this Bible study include:

—Use of scripture passages printed on hand-outs for each participant

—Scripture references given in the *Confession of Faith* printed on newsprint for viewing by the entire group

Perceptions of the duties of elders and deacons may vary widely according to what individuals believe is expected of them. The following activity will give participants an opportunity to identify and discuss these perceptions in relation to their own expectations and in relation to what they believe the minister and congregation expect of them.

Activities

Give each participant three index cards. Using one card for each point, the participant should describe what he/she believes are

1. the duties of the office of elder or deacon
2. expectations of the minister
3. expectations of the congregation
(10 minutes)

In groups of three or four, the participants discuss the individual perceptions listed on the cards, noting similarities and differences. If both elders and deacons are involved in the total group, elders should be grouped with elders and deacons with deacons.

With all the participants together, ask a spokesperson from each small group to report the perceptions. Be sure that each of the three types of expectations are covered in the discussion. (20 minutes)

As an alternative activity, give each participant a newsprint sheet and felt-tip marker with directions to fold the sheet lengthwise into three sections. The perceptions of the individual, minister and congregation would then be listed in the three sections of the sheet. When the listing is completed, the sheets would be displayed to give all participants the opportunity to read what others have listed.

The discussion of duties as perceived by individuals should be followed by a study of what is stated in the *Constitution*. In the next activity, participants will compare their perceptions with the duties listed in the *Constitution*.

Activity

Distribute copies of the *Confession of Faith* to participants, directing them to turn to the pertinent sections of the Constitution (Section 2.70 for elders or 2.80 for deacons). If copies of the *Confession of Faith* are not available, preprint the sections on individual sheets or on newsprint sheets.

Compare the individual perceptions with the Constitution listings, noting any significant differences. (15 minutes)

ESTABLISHING PRIORITIES AND DEVELOPING GOALS

After church officers have a good understanding of their duties, they should establish priorities and identify the goals which will allow them to fulfill their responsibilities. In the following activity, participants will formulate more specific plans to meet the duties of their office.

Activity

Distribute copies of the form, "Plans for Fulfilling the Duties of My Office." There are separate forms for elders and deacons. Review each section, explaining the significance of each column:

* Column one contains the duties listed in the Constitution. Encourage the listing of additional duties which have emerged in the discussion of individual perceptions.
* Column two requires decision on priorities. Each duty is to be given a priority by circling a number with 1 as a high priority, 2 as a medium priority and 3 as a low priority.
* Column three gives space for each officer to list goals for fulfilling duties. (10 minutes)

After participants have completed their forms, organize groups of three to discuss their individual plans. Following the small group review, the entire group should repeat the process so that ideas may be expanded or clarified. Encourage responses by asking such questions as

1. Which duties were listed as having high priority?
2. Which were listed as least important?
3. Were the goals specific or general?

Individual goals may sometimes require modification or even replacement by goals developed by the full session, diaconate or congregation. (15 minutes)

FULFILLING GOALS

It is sometimes difficult for individuals to carry out plans because they lack knowledge of resources available to them. The following activity should help church officers become aware of those resources.

Activity

Divide a newsprint sheet into two columns; label one column *Printed Resources* and the other column *Human Resources*. Ask participants to brainstorm ideas of available resources, indicating to which church officer duty the resource would relate. Refer to items on "Plans for Fulfilling the Duties of My Office." For example, *The Confession of Faith* would be a printed resource for gaining knowledge of the doctrine and government of the church (item six, form for elders). Another elder or deacon would be an example of a human resource for visiting people in their homes (item three, form for elders).

When the group completes brainstorming, suggest participants copy any pertinent ideas on their individual planning forms. (15 minutes)

EVALUATION

Give each participants an index card and ask for completion of this statement: "One new thing I learned about the duties of elders and deacons is _____" (5 minutes)

Bibliography

Church Officer Pre-Ordination Curriculum, Unit III, Duties of Elders and Deacons, The Geneva Press, 1975.

The Noble Task, by Andrew A. Jumper, John Knox Press, 1965.

Chosen To Serve, by Andrew A. Jumper, John Knox Press, 1966.

The Confession of Faith and Government of the Cumberland Presbyterian Church and Second Cumberland Presbyterian Church, 1984.

Consider Your Ministry, A Study Manual for New Officers, edited by W. Ben Lane, Geneva Press, 1981.

Strengthening Personal Faith Experience

Focus

Persons who are elected to the office of elder or deacon are called upon to exemplify sound faith, "deep abiding faith in Jesus Christ, whose example in ministry they follow" (*Constitution*, Section 2.73, 2.83).

At times, persons may hesitate about serving as a church officer, perhaps needing some reassurance that their faith experiences are strong enough to equip them adequately for the task.

This training is structured to give elders and deacons an in-depth look at their individual faith experience. The intention is not to judge any person's faith as superior to another's but, in the relating and reflecting of experience, to gain strength and confidence in the ability to serve.

Time Requirement: About 2 hours

Objectives

The participants will:
1. reflect upon their life experiences in terms of their own faith;
2. explore these faith experiences in light of scripture;
3. describe individual experiences to the group;
4. plan devotional/worship models which may be used in session and/or diaconate meetings.

Preparation

1. Obtain supplies: marking pens, index cards, masking tape, newsprint sheets, paper and pencils.
2. Duplicate resource sheet B-1 (prayer/litany) or obtain other worship aids as needed, resource sheet B-2 (My Faith Journey) and resource sheet B-3 (Suggestions for Developing Devotional Models).
3. Print objectives on newsprint sheet.
4. Write "How has my faith journey prepared me to serve as a church officer?" at the top of a newsprint sheet.
5. Write Scripture references Romans 12:1-16, I Corinthians 12:4-12 and Ephesians 4:1-16 at the top of newsprint sheets, one on each sheet.

Procedure

INTRODUCTION

Begin the training with a 10-minute period of worship. Before the worship begins, spend a few minutes making introductions and encouraging a relaxed atmosphere. Suggestions for leading the group in worship include:

—Use a prayer, hymn or scripture reading relating to the meaning of faith
—Use a prayer/litany (see resource sheet B-1)
—Ask each person to think of a word or phrase associated with faith and to share the word/phrase with the group. Write the words/phrases on a newsprint sheet displayed to the group as a visual aid for worship. Ask each participant to pray silently for guidance in exploring the aspects of faith indicated by the expressions written on the sheet.

Refer to the focus of the study and review the objectives for the training (written on newsprint and displayed to the group). Give time for questions and clarification of the objectives. (5 minutes)

REFLECTION OF FAITH EXPERIENCES

It is not easy to look inward and reflect on experiences which have shaped our spiritual selves. It can, however, be a helpful activity in strengthening faith. The following activity gives participants a structure for individual reflection.

Activity

Give each participant the resource sheet, "My Faith Journey." Ask each to work individually to complete the chart by following the instructions. (10 minutes)

In pairs or groups of three, give participants an opportunity to describe as much of their faith journey as they wish. (5 to 10 minutes)

Reassemble the group. Summarize

the activity by asking for responses to the question, "How has my faith journey prepared me to serve as a church officer?" Write the responses on a newsprint sheet and post on the wall. (10 minutes)

RELATING EXPERIENCES TO SCRIPTURE

Three passages of scripture are suggested for study which relate to the importance of personal commitment, the diversity of Christian experience and the unity of the church: Romans 12:1-16, I Corinthians 12:4-12 and Ephesians 4:1-16.

Activity

Divide participants into three groups. Assign each group one of the suggested scripture passages. Give each group a newsprint sheet with instructions to outline briefly the main points of the passage, highlighting key words and phrases. (10 minutes)

When the groups have completed their assignments, post the newsprint sheets on the wall in view of everyone. Ask someone from each group to review the information on its sheet, giving time for anyone to ask questions or make additional comments about each passage. Summarize by discussing the question, "What are the implications in these scriptures for serving as church officers?" (10 to 15 minutes)

PLANNING DEVOTIONAL/WORSHIP TIMES

The *Constitution* states that "all meetings of judicatories shall be opened and closed with prayer" (Section 3.05). Many church officers believe it is important to have a more extensive devotional/worship time at the beginning or close of meetings. Because some persons are uneasy about leading in prayer or giving devo-

tions, spend some time soliciting such concerns from the group. These questions are suggested:

—How do I choose a scripture reading?
—What are some ways to study a Bible passage?
—Is it permissable to use a printed prayer?
—Is it necessary to use a hymn?
—Should the group be asked to participate in some way?

As the concerns are stated, write them on a newsprint sheet for everyone to see. (5 minutes)

Activity

Assign participants to groups of three or four to work on a two-part task.

Ask each group to discuss the concerns listed on the newsprint. Respond to as many as possible with specific, positive suggestions. The suggestions should be written on the upper half of the newsprint sheet. (5 to 10 minutes)

Direct each small group to develop a devotional model which could be used in a session or diaconate meeting. The group may create its own model or use suggestions from resource sheet B-3 as a guide. Ask each group to write its devotional model on the lower half of their newsprint sheet. Post all the sheets on the wall. Give participants time to circulate, read the information and copy suggestions for future use. (10 minutes)

CLOSING AND EVALUATION

Ask one of the groups to volunteer to use one of the devotional models for a closing worship time. (5 minutes)

Ask participants to respond (on index cards) to these questions:

1. Which part of the workshop was most helpful?
2. Which part was least helpful? (3 minutes)

Work of the Session and Diaconate

The Cumberland Presbyterian Church and the Second Cumberland Presbyterian Church are governed by representative bodies, one of which is the session. As described in the *Confession of Faith*, the responsibility of these representative bodies is to determine matters of faith and practice and government, propose forms of worship and witness, exercise discipline and resolve appeals brought before them (*Confession of Faith*, Sections 5.34 and 5.35).

The diaconate is not one of the representative bodies in the judicatories of the church. However, congregations may elect and ordain deacons.

In this two-part training, elders and deacons study their corporate responsibilities.

Part I deals with the work of the session.
Time Requirement: 1 to 1½ hours
Part II deals with the work of the diaconate.
Time Requirement: ¾ to 1 hour.

WORK OF THE SESSION

Objectives
Participants will:
1. identify the corporate responsibilities of the session;
2. put these responsibilities into categories which represent different areas of the life and witness of the congregation;
3. match areas of responsibility with individual interests and abilities.

Preparation
1. Gather resources: copies of the *Confession of Faith* and session minutes.
2. Obtain supplies: marking pens, newsprint, masking tape, pencils, chalkboard.
3. Duplicate resource sheets C-1 (Is This Our Responsibility?), C-2 (Sample Listing of Items from Session Minutes) and C-3 (Corporate Responsibilities of the Session).
4. Prepare charts for steps "Analyzing Information from Small Groups" and "Choosing Areas of Responsibility."

Procedure

INTRODUCTION

As leader, you may wish to say to the group: "Suppose you are about to attend a session meeting for the first time as a new elder. That may, in fact, be your situation today or those of you who have served previously may recall your first meeting. You may be somewhat apprehensive because you are not sure just what your duties are or what is expected of you as a session member. You have read the information in the *Confession of Faith and Constitution* relating to the work of the session, but you are still uncertain how the responsibilities listed there are actually carried out in real situations. The following activities will help introduce you to your role as a session member."

Refer to the focus of the study and review the objectives (written on newsprint and displayed to the group). (5 minutes)

Activity
DETERMINING RESPONSIBILITIES
Ask each participant to complete resource sheet C-1, "Is This Our Responsibility?" Make sure everyone understands the directions at the top of the sheet; explain that the answers will be checked later. (5 minutes)

Activity
CATEGORIZING ITEMS FROM MINUTES OF THE SESSION
The group may work from either of these two resources:
1. The sample listing of items from a session meeting, given on resource sheet C-2;
2. Minutes for an actual meeting.

To use resource sheet C-2, divide group into pairs or groups of three. Assign each pair or group an equal share of the items listed on C-2; give each pair or group resource sheet C-3.

The C-3 guide sheet divides the session's responsibilities, as listed in the *Constitution*, into four major categories. Ask each group to identify and label its assigned items according to a category on the guide sheet. For example, the action of the session in regard to receiving new church members would come under category II, Administration. (10 minutes)

If using actual session minutes, each group should be given a copy of minutes and instructed to identify three to five items of business. Each group would then categorize the items using C-3 as suggested above.

Activity
ANALYZING INFORMATION FROM SMALL GROUPS

Divide a chalkboard or large newsprint sheet into a four-section chart. Assign each section one of the four major category headings from resource sheet C-3.

Reassemble the participants. Ask someone from each work group to report the results of their categorizing action from session minutes. As each item is identified by category, write the item under that category on the large composite chart. The composite listing will be easier to analyze if the item is written out rather than just identified by item number.

When the composite listing is complete, the group should discuss the results, using the following questions as a basis for discussion:

—Under which category are most of the items listed?
—Referring to the corporate responsibilities resource sheet C-1, are there areas which are not receiving attention? If so, what are the possible reasons? Is most of the session activity focused under any one area of responsibility?
—Are there items from the minutes which do not seem to fit under any category? Are these the responsibility of the session?

Note: The preceding discussion needs to take into consideration whether the church is a single governing board or both a session and a diaconate. (15 minutes)

Activity
CHOOSING AREAS OF RESPONSIBILITY

Give each participant resource sheet C-3. Ask each to review the sheet and then identify at least three items of responsibility which most closely fit his/her particular interests and abilities.

Using a four-section chart on chalkboard or newsprint, tabulate these preferences. Use this composite of preferences to identify strengths and weaknesses in the group as a whole. If this activity is being used by officers from different churches, the tabulation could be used to suggest where sessions in general place priorities and which responsibilities tend to receive little or no attention. (10 minutes)

CLOSING AND EVALUATION

Refer to the resource sheet C-1, "Is This Our Responsibility?" used to introduce the study. Ask the participants to recheck their responses to determine if they would make any changes as a result of the study. Give the correct matching for the items on the sheet. Discuss any comments or questions.

Evaluate by asking participants to discuss any insights they received which they believe will better enable them to perform as session members. (10 minutes)

Note: Answers for resource sheet C-1 are as follows:

1-i, 2-a, 3-g, 4-e, 5-h, 6-c, 7-j, 8-d, 9-b, 10-f

Bibliography

The Confession of Faith and Government of the Cumberland Presbyterian Church and Second Cumberland Presbyterian Church, 1984.

Work of the Session and the Diaconate, Unit 1, Continuing Education Series, The Geneva Press, 1975.

WORK OF THE DIACONATE

Objectives
Participants will:
1. identify the responsibilities given in the *Constitution;*
2. outline current practices;
3. describe the relationship between the session and the diaconate.

Preparation

1. Gather resources: copies of the *Confession of Faith* and minutes of meetings of the diaconate.
2. Obtain supplies: marking pens, newsprint, masking tape, pencils, chalkboard.
3. Print objectives on newsprint sheet.
4. Duplicate resource sheet C-4 (Corporate Responsibilities of diaconate).
5. Prepare newsprint chart with three sections labeled Administration, Ministry and Service and Education.

Procedure

INTRODUCTION

In some congregations there is only one governing body, the session. Many churches, however, have both a session and a diaconate. Where both exist, there is sometimes a lack of understanding of the responsibilities of the diaconate and the relationship between it and the session.

The following activities will help participants broaden their understanding of the work of the diaconate.

Activity

DEFINING TASKS

Briefly review the objectives (listed on newsprint) with the group. Working in pairs or groups of three, ask each small group to list the tasks usually done by the deacons. An example of a task is receiving the offering during worship. (5 minutes)

Reassemble the entire group and ask someone from each small group to report the items it listed. As these are reported, make a composite listing on newsprint or chalkboard, eliminating any duplicate items. When reporting is completed, ask if there are any other additions to the list. (10 minutes)

Activity

IDENTIFYING RESPONSIBILITIES

Provide each participant with resource sheet C-4 or the *Confession of Faith* can be used to study this information, found in sections 2.81 and 2.82 in the Constitution.

Lead the participants in comparing the newsprint list with the list of responsibilities in the *Constitution*. These questions can be used to guide the analysis:

- Are there items on the newsprint list which do not seem to fall within the areas of responsibility given in the *Constitution*?
- Can any of these tasks be done by the deacons under the direction of the session?
- Are there any items which should never be assigned to deacons?
- Does the *Constitution* list areas of responsibility which do not appear on the group's listing? If so, why has this occurred? (10 minutes)

In summarizing the discussion, emphasize these points concerning the relationship between the session and the diaconate:

1. Even though certain responsibilities are assigned to them in the *Constitution*, the deacons are always responsible to the session (Section 4.5h in the *Constitution* states that the session is to examine the proceedings and supervise work of the deacons).
2. The responsibility of the deacons may be limited but that does not mean or imply that their work is unimportant. The relationship is simply that the diaconate is under the authority of the session. (5 minutes)

Activity

OUTLINING CURRENT PRACTICES

Use the newsprint chart with section headings of Administration, Ministry and Service, and Education to outline current practices of boards of deacons. This activity will give a picture of where most time and effort is concentrated and which areas of responsibility are neglected. Either of the following methods may be used:

1. Compile a list of actions from minutes of meetings of the diaconate; the group can then categorize the listed items according to the sections on the chart.
2. Using a list of responsibilities compiled in the first two activities, ask the group to assign each item to a category on the chart. Before using the list, be sure to eliminate any items determined not to be the responsibility of the deacons.

If the group is large, consider separating participants into small groups. Divide the list of activities among the groups and ask them to label their items according to the chart headings. Each group can then report to the reassembled group, placing items in the appropriate categories.

Discuss and evaluate what the chart reveals, based on these questions:

- Which area receives the most attention?
- In view of the responsibilities given in the *Constitution*, which area(s) should be expanded?

(15 minutes)

CLOSING AND EVALUATION

In summarizing the study, refer to the fact that the office of deacon is rooted in Scripture. The preamble to the *Constitution* states that "in addition to the office of elder, the New Testament refers to a group of lay leaders called deacons who had a special responsibility in the care of the poor and others in need." Call attention to the clear emphasis placed on service. Emphasize that deacons have very important tasks to perform and may need to re-evaluate their understanding of their responsibility.

Ask the participants to evaluate by responding to the question, "How can the information gained from this study better prepare me to serve as a member of the diaconate?" (5 minutes)

Team Building

Focus

Church officers do not serve in isolation. They are part of a team of persons who care for and support each other in making decisions and carrying out plans. The effectiveness of the team can make a difference in how individual members feel about being a part of it and in the quality of leadership the team provides for the congregation. It is vitally important that elders and deacons feel that they are not alone in fulfilling the responsibilities of the office they have assumed.

In this training, participants will explore what it means to be an effective team member.

Time Requirement: 2 to 2½ hours

Objectives

At the end of the study, participants will:
1. be better personally acquainted with each other.
2. understand how a group functions effectively.
3. have improved interpersonal communication skills.

Preparation

1. Obtain supplies: newsprint, various colored marking pens, masking tape, sheets of light-colored construction paper, cardboard and envelopes for constructing "Broken Squares" activity, index cards, pencils.
2. Write objectives on newsprint sheet.
3. Prepare for "Broken Squares" activity (see Resource Sheet D-1): one set of instructions for each group, one set of instructions for each observer and one set of broken squares for each group.

Procedure

GETTING ACQUAINTED

Briefly review the objectives, adding or clarifying as needed.

A group of church officers may meet regularly and still not be personally acquainted. Some sessions and diaconates are so large that responsibilities are divided among committees, thus limiting personal interaction. Many sessions and diaconates operate on a rotation system which each year involves new persons who may not be well known to other group members. There may be other reasons why church officers need to spend some time in simply becoming better acquainted.

The following activities encourage participants to get to know each other better. (5 minutes)

Activity

Divide the group into pairs. In a 5-minute period, each person is to discover as much personal information as possible about his/her partner. Following the allotted time, each person then presents her/his partner to the group, sharing as much information as can be recalled. (20 minutes).

Activity

Form the group into two concentric circles, inner and outer, with participants facing each other. The persons in the inner circle talk to those in the outer circle about statements (announced by the leader), using two minutes for each statement. After each two-minute segment, the outer circle shifts counterclockwise. After all the statements have been responded to by the inner circle, the same process is repeated with the outer circle doing the talking. Sessions comprised of fewer than five members may use this activity by working in pairs instead of circles.

STATEMENTS for INNER CIRCLE:
1. If I could visit any place in the world on vacation _____
2. If I only had one more day to live _____
3. The thing I fear the most is _____

STATEMENTS for OUTER CIRCLE:
1. The greatest value in my life at the moment is _____
2. The thing that gives me the greatest satisfaction is _____
3. The time I feel most alone is _____

(15 minutes)

Give each person a sheet of light-colored construction paper and a marking pen. Participants are asked to:

1. Print their name in the center of the sheet.
2. In the upper left corner, write or draw two things they are good at doing (such as singing, sports, etcetera).
3. In the upper right corner, name or draw their favorite food.
4. In the lower left corner, write how they seem to themselves (timid, aggressive, caring, etcetera).
5. In the lower right corner describe how they think others see them (friendly, fun-loving, etcetera).

When the information sheets are completed, ask participants to hold the sheets so they can be seen by others, walking around the room and talking to each other about their information sheets. (20 to 25 minutes)

GROUP FUNCTIONING

Another step in helping church members to become a team is to improve their understanding of how a group functions effectively. Use the following activities to help participants expand their understanding of group dynamics.

Activity

Ask participants to suggest elements of effective group functioning (common goals, trust, cooperation, openness, acceptance, etcetera). As the suggestions are made, list them on newsprint. Accept all suggestions, eliminating only those that are obvious duplicates. (5 minutes)

Divide into groups of three or four; if there are fewer than six persons, remain in one group. Give each small group an equal share of the suggestions from the newsprint sheet. Ask each group to identify the implications of the suggestions for the church session or diaconate. For example, when there is trust among group members, there is greater freedom to express joy, fears, doubts and ideas. (15 minutes)

Reassemble the group. Ask someone from each small group to report ideas from its discussion. (15 minutes)

Activity

Divide into groups of six participants each. If there are not enough participants to form more than one group, assign more than one observer/judge to the group. There will be five players and an observer/judge in each group. Each group should sit at tables spaced far enough apart so the groups cannot observe each other's activities.

The leader begins with a discussion of the meaning of cooperation, soliciting from the groups suggestions of what is essential in successful group cooperation. These suggestions may be listed on the board. The leader then indicates the groups will conduct an experiment to test their suggestions. After this preliminary discussion, the leader designates the observer/judge for each group of five players. Each observer is given a copy of his/her instructions. The leader gives each group a packet and asks it to distribute the envelopes it contains. The envelopes are to remain unopened until the signal is given to begin.

The leader distributes a copy of the instructions to each group, then reads the instructions, calling for questions to assure understanding. The leader gives a signal to begin and allows 15 minutes for the task.

When the groups have completed the task, the leader engages the groups in a discussion of the experience. The discussion should focus on feelings, going beyond merely relating experiences and general observations. (5 minutes)

INSTRUCTIONS TO THE GROUPS

Provide each group a copy of the following instructions:

"In this packet there are five envelopes, each of which contains pieces of cardboard for forming squares. When the leader gives the signal to begin, the task of your group is to form five squares of equal size. The task will not be completed until each individual has before him/her a perfect square of the same size as that held by others.

"Specific limitations are imposed upon your group during this activity:

1. No member may speak.
2. No member may ask another member for a

card or in any way signal that another person is to give him a card.

3. Members may, however, give cards to other members.

The leader should ask, "Are the instructions clear?" and respond to any questions. Then the leader gives the signal, "Begin working."

INSTRUCTIONS TO OBSERVER/JUDGE

Provide a copy of the following rules to each observer/judge:

"Your job is part observer and part judge. Make sure each participant observes the rules:

1. No talking, pointing, or any other kind of communication will be allowed among the five people in your group.
2. Participants may give pieces to other participants but may not take pieces from other members.
3. Participants may not simply throw their pieces into the center for others to take; they have to give the pieces directly to one person.
4. It is permissable for a member to give away all the pieces to his own puzzle, even if he/she has already formed a square.

"Do your best to strictly enforce these rules. As an observer you may want to look for some of the following:

1. Who is willing to give away pieces of the puzzle?
2. Did anyone finish his/her puzzle and then remove him/herself from the struggles of the rest of the group?
3. Is there anyone who struggles with his/her pieces, yet is unwilling to give any or all of them away?
4. How many people are actively engaged in mentally putting the pieces together?
5. Periodically, check the level of frustration and anxiety: who is pulling his/her hair out?
6. Was there any critical turning point at which time the group began to cooperate?
7. Did anyone try to violate the rules by talking or pointing as a means of helping other members solve their puzzle?"

(Source of activity: *A Handbook of Structured Experiences for Human Relations Training,* Volume I, J. William Pfeiffer and John E. Jones, Editors, University Associates Press, Box 615, Iowa City, Iowa.)

The following summarizes the section on group functioning:

"In all human interactions there are two major ingredients—*content* and *process.* The first deals with the subject matter or the task upon which the group is working. In most interactions, the focus of attention of all persons is on the content. The second ingredient, process, is concerned with what is happening between and to group members while the group is working. Group process or dynamics deals with such things as morale, feeling, tone, atmosphere, influence, participation, styles of influence, leadership struggles, conflict, competition, cooperation, etcetera.

"In most interactions very little attention is paid to process, even when it is the major cause of ineffective group action. Sensitivity to process will better enable one to diagnose group problems early and deal with them more effectively. Since these processes are present in all groups, awareness of them will enhance a person's worth to a group and enable him or her to be a more effective group participant."

(Source: *The 1972 Annual Handbook for Group Facilitators,* edited by William Pfeiffer and John Jones, University Associates, Iowa City, Iowa.)

COMMUNICATION

Members of any team need to know and practice effective communication skills. An inability to communicate or a breakdown in communication between members of a session or diaconate can cause inefficiency or even conflict within the group. In the following activities participants practice good communication techniques. The first two activities illustrate non-listening barriers which prevent good understanding between persons.

Activity

Divide the group into groups of four or five participants. Each group selects one person to present a one-minute summary of his/her life from birth to present. While the speaker tries very hard to keep the attention of the other participants, they become "non-listeners" and do whatever they can to *not* listen to the speaker.

If time permits, give each participant an opportunity to be the speaker and to experience the frustration of saying something important and not having anyone listen. (10 minutes)

Activity

Organize participants in pairs. Give each person an index card and pencil. Ask each person to write six or eight sentences, all related to a single topic of his/her choice. No one should know what his/her partner has written. When the lists are completed, partners alternate reading one sentence at a time, using a dramatic manner. The exercise should readily demonstrate the futility of word exchanges in which neither party is tuned in to or interested in the other's message. (10 minutes)

Activity

"To listen effectively and healingly is an act of well-developed faith." (*Author unknown*) On a newsprint sheet, write the following helps and non-helps in listening in two columns. Briefly review the information for the group.

Helps in Listening	Non-Helps in Listening
• Sitting close without touching	• Keeping distance
• Facing each other	• Turning away
• Touching when appropriate (rare)	• Touching in appropriately
• Sitting in a receptive posture	• Pointing finger
• Making appropriate gestures	• Making distracting gestures
• Staying awake	• Yawning or dozing
• Keeping good eye contact without staring	• Closing eyes
	• Tightening lips or crossing arms

The Positive Focus Game

Form participants into groups of three. Provide each group with a question or controversial statement which will elicit a values-related response. Example: "Do you feel the church should be involved in political issues?" Allow a few minutes for persons to make notes to assist them in responding.

Within each group, one person agrees to be the focus of the group for five minutes. The focus person briefly states his/her reaction to the question or statement. The two other persons then try to find out more about the focus person's opinion by following these three rules:

1. *Rule of Focusing:* The focus person is to be the absolute center of attention for the entire five minutes. The remaining two must do nothing to turn attention to themselves. They cannot debate, disagree, express their opinions or talk about their experiences. They must repress their ideas and opinions, expressing them only when they are in the focus person role.

2. *Rule of Drawing Out:* The two inquirers do everything they can to draw out the focus person and find out as much as possible about what he/she thinks and why. Questions are a primary way to elicit the focus person's thoughts and reasoning. The questions should be phrased to help the focus person clarify the ideas for himself and for the inquirers; the questions should not probe beyond what the person apparently wants to reveal. Further, questions should lead the focus person in the direction that really helps him/her clarify his thinking; the questions should not lead in a direction the inquirers may think it should go. If the focus person feels the questions probe too deeply or lead in the wrong direction, he/she should say so.

3. *Rule of Acceptance:* The two inquirers should try to accept the focus person completely and let him/her know they are trying to understand his/her point of view. They do not have to agree with what the person says but they must agree with his/her right to say it. Even if they disagree with what he/she is saying, they should give only positive feedback such as "I understand what you are saying" and "I can see how you feel that way" or just nodding or smiling. It is difficult not to give negative feedback when you strongly disagree with someone but it becomes easier each time the game is played. Inquirers should be careful they do not subtly convey negative reaction through frowning, voice tone or wording of questions.

Stop the groups at the end of five minutes and ask them to evaluate briefly how well each person has followed the rules of the game. If time permits, give each person in each trio an opportunity to be the focus person. After everyone has played, ask for responses to this question: "What does the Focus Game suggest to us about listening to others, eliciting their opinion and accepting their opinion?"

(Source: *Personalizing Education*, Values Clarification and Beyond, by Leland W. Howe and

Mary M. Howe, Hart Publishing Co., Inc., N.Y., 1975.)

CLOSING AND EVALUATION

Refer to the focus of the training and reemphasize the importance of church officer groups' working together effectively as persons who care for and support each other in decision-making and carrying out plans. Use one of the following scripture passages as a concluding thought: Ephesians 4:1-16, I Corinthians 13 or Romans 12:3-13. (5 minutes)

Give each person an index card and pencil. Direct participants to draw three lines horizontally across the card, labeling the lines *a*, *b*, and *c* to correspond with each of the objectives of the training. Each line represents a continuum ranging from 1 (low success in meeting objective) at the left to 10 (great success) at the right. Ask participants to rate the objectives by placing a check mark somewhere on each line. Collect the completed evaluations. (5 minutes)

Bibliography

A Handbook of Structured Experiences for Human Relations Training, Vol. 1, by J. William Pfeiffer and John E. Jones, Editors, University Associates Press, Iowa City, Iowa.

The 1972 Annual Handbook for Group Facilitators, edited by William Pfeiffer and John Jones, University Associates, Iowa City, Iowa.

Personalizing Education, Values Clarification and Beyond, Leland W. Howe and Mary M. Howe, Hart Publishing Co., Inc., N.Y., 1975.

Organizing the Session and Diaconate

Focus

The *Constitution* is not very specific about the organizational structure of church sessions and diaconates. Although a basic structure of church sessions is outlined in Sections 4.1-4.7 of the *Constitution,* most details are left to be determined by the congregation, according to its size and needs. Likewise, if the congregation has elected deacons, it determines the organizational structure of that group.

Because the memberships of both groups change periodically, newly-elected officers should be informed about the structure and rules of procedure for the groups.

In this training, participants will review information which can help them be better organized for their task. Part I is for use by the session and Part II by the diaconate.

Time Requirement: 1½ to 2 hours

```
ELDERS

Objectives
Participants will:
1. identify statements in the Constitu-
   tion which relate to organizing a
   session;
2. describe the organizational struc-
   ture of their own session;
3. develop a model for a standard of
   procedure for the session.
```

Preparation

1. Gather resources: copies of the *Confession of Faith and Constitution.*
2. Obtain supplies: pencils, chalkboard or newsprint and marking pens.
3. Duplicate resource sheets E-1 (True-False Quiz), E-2 (*Constitution* Requirements), E-3 (Organizational Structure: Session) and E-4 (Standard of Procedure Outline Form) for each participant.

Procedure

INTRODUCTION

Explain the purpose of the study, referring to the focus statements. The study is not intended to identify any one pattern of organization as "right" and another as "wrong" (except when contrary to the standard of organization in the *Constitution).* Emphasize, however, that poor organization and ignorance of procedure can contribute to confusion, conflict and a generally ineffective ministry.

After making certain all members of the group are acquainted, briefly review the objectives. The objectives may be revised or expanded by the group as needed. (5 minutes)

Activity

Distribute the True-False Quiz (resource sheet E-1) to each participant. Explain that responses to the statements should be indicated with a T for true and F for false. Announce that the correct answer will be given and discussed later. (5 minutes)

USING THE CONSTITUTION

Although the *Constitution* isn't specific on how the session is organized, elders should be familiar with the basic structure as outlined in the *Constitution.* The following activity allows examination of the structure and comparison with current practices of the session.

Activity

Give each person a copy of the *Confession of Faith and Constitution* (or resource sheet E-2) and Organizational Structure: Session (resource sheet E-3). Ask participants to work alone or in pairs to fill in the information on E-3. Make sure the worksheet directions are understood. (15 minutes)

Bring participants together to discuss their work. These points should be emphasized:

1. There may be differences among congregations on how their respective sessions are organized.
2. Each session needs to establish rules by which to organize and conduct business; the rules must be consistent with the requirements in the *Constitution.*
3. The rules of procedure (called a Standard of Procedure) should be

in written form and available to each session member.

4. As Moderator of the session, the minister in charge has an extraordinary responsibility to understand fully the organizational structure of the session and its standard of procedure; he/she must be prepared to carry out the duties of presiding officer.

As items on the worksheet are discussed, discrepancies may be discovered between actual practices and the information in the *Constitution*. Any such differences should be discussed thoroughly. Invite suggestions on how practices could be brought into line with the Constitution's direction.

Summarize by asking participants to review the True-False Quiz taken earlier. Ask them if they would now change any answers in light of the activity just finished. Give the correct answers and discuss any further questions or comments. (15 minutes)

(Answers to Quiz: 1.F, 2.T, 3.T, 4.F, 5.T, 6.T, 7.F, 8.T, 9.T, 10.F)

DEVELOPING A STANDARD OF PROCEDURE

Many sessions are organized only in a general way and do not have a written standard of procedure. In the next activity, participants develop a basic model which can be adapted for use by a local session.

Note: The activity can be used as a review for sessions which already have a written standard of procedure.

Activity

If necessary, explain the meaning of a standard of procedure. Give each participant a copy of the Stardard of Procedure Outline Form (resource sheet E-4). Divide the group into groups of three or four. Assign each group a share of the items on the form; ask each group to discuss its assigned items and to write suggestions on the form. Example: Items I (Officers) and II (Duties of Officers) would be assigned to one group. The group might suggest that officers would be a moderator, a moderator pro tem and a clerk (and treasurer, in congregations without a diaconate). The group would then

briefly describe duties for each officer. (10 to 15 minutes)

After the groups complete their assignments, reassemble. As each group reports its results, write a composite of the suggestions on the chalkboard or newsprint sheet. Encourage questions and accept additions to all parts of the outline. Give particular attention to duties of the moderator and clerk. Suggest that each participant complete his/her outline from the composite one. (30 minutes)

CLOSING AND EVALUATION

Conclude with the reading of Acts 16:4-5 and 20:28, followed by prayer.

Evaluate by asking participants to respond, either orally or in writing, to the question: "How has this workshop helped me be better prepared to serve as an elder?" (5 minutes)

Bibliography

The Noble Task, the Elder, by Andrew A. Jumper, John Knox Press, 1974.

The Office of Clerk of Session, by Frank M. Beatty, John Knox Press, 1963.

The Cumberland Presbyterian Digest, 1975, by Charles Hinkley Smartt, Frontier Press, Memphis, TN.

The Confession of Faith and Government of the Cumberland Presbyterian Church and Second Cumberland Presbyterian Church, 1984.

DEACONS

Objectives

Participants will:

1. identify statements in the *Constitution* which relate to organizing a diaconate;
2. describe the organizational structure of their own diaconate;
3. develop a model for a standard of procedure for the diaconate.

Preparation

1. Gather resources: copies of *Confession of Faith and Constitution.*
2. Obtain supplies: pencils, chalkboard or newsprint and marking pen.
3. Duplicate resource sheets E-1 (True-False Quiz), E-2 (Constitution Requirements), E-4

(Standard of Procedure Outline Form) and E-5 (Organizational Structure: Deacons) for each participant.

Procedure

INTRODUCTION

Refer to the focus of the study and explain its purpose. Explain that although all churches do not elect deacons, good organization is critical to those which do. Patterns of organization will vary according to size and needs. Emphasize the importance of understanding that the diaconate is under the supervision of and responsible to the church session and is not a court of the church.

After introductions, briefly review the objectives. They may be revised or expanded by the group as needed. (5 minutes)

Activity

Distribute the True-False Quiz (E-1) to each participant. Give directions for the activity and explain that the correct answers will be announced and discussed later. (5 minutes)

USING THE *CONSTITUTION*

Specific information on diaconate organization is very limited. Deacons should, however, be familiar with the available information. In the following activity, participants study the information and compare it with current practices in diaconate organization.

Activity

Give each person a *Confession of Faith and Constitution* (or a copy of resource sheet E-2) and resource sheet E-5 (Organizational Structure: Deacons). Suggest they work individually or in pairs to fill in the information on the worksheet, making sure directions are understood. (15 to 20 minutes)

Bring the participants together to discuss their responses on the worksheet. Highlight these points:
1. Differences may exist among congregations as to diaconate organization.
2. Rules are needed for organizing and conducting business.
3. A written standard of procedure should be developed.
4. A full understanding of the rela-

tionship between the diaconate and session is important.

As items on the worksheet are presented, discuss any questions which arise concerning current practices. Summarize by referring to the True-False Quiz taken earlier in the study. Ask participants if they would now change any of their answers in view of the activity just completed. Give the correct answers to the quiz and discuss any additional questions. (10 to 15 minutes)

(Answers to Quiz: 1.F, 2.T, 3.T, 4.F, 5.T, 6.T, 7.F, 8.T, 9.T, 10.F)

DEVELOPING A STANDARD OF PROCEDURE

Like church sessions, diaconates need a written standard of procedure to function effectively and properly. In the following activity, participants develop a basic model which can be adapted by a particular church.

Note: The activity can be used as a review for diaconates which already have a written standard of procedure.

Activity

Explain the meaning of a standard of procedure. Give each participant a Standard of Procedure Outline Form (E-4). Divide the group into smaller groups. Assign each a share of the items on the outline. Ask each group to discuss its assigned items and write on the form suggestions for that part of the standard of procedure. Example: Items I (Officers) and II (Duties of Officers) would be assigned to one group. It might suggest that the diaconate officers should be a chairperson, a vice-chairperson, a secretary and a treasurer-bookkeeper. Then the group would briefly describe the duties of each officer. (10 to 15 minutes)

After the groups complete their assignments, reassemble. As each group reports its results, write a composite of the suggestions on the chalkboard or newsprint. Encourage questions and additions to the full outline. Give particular attention to the duties of the treasurer. Suggest that each participant complete his/her copy of the outline from the composite one. (30 minutes)

CLOSING AND EVALUATION

Conclude with a reading of I Timothy 3:13; 4:6-10, followed by prayer.

Evaluate by asking participants to respond, orally or in writing, to the question: "How has this workshop helped me be better prepared to serve as a deacon?" (5 minutes)

Bibliography

The Confession of Faith and Government of the Cumberland Presbyterian church and Second Cumberland Presbyterian Church, 1984.

The Cumberland Presbyterian Digest, 1975, by Charles Hinkley Smartt, Frontier Press, Memphis, TN.

Chosen to Serve, The Deacon, by Andrew A. Jumper, John Knox Press, 1961.

Knowing the Congregation

Focus

It is the church session's responsibility to lead the members of the congregation in all the ministries of the church (*Constitution*, Section 2.51). The session is also charged with the pastoral oversight of the congregation (*Constitution*, Section 4.5).

In order to meet effectively those responsibilities, certain information about the congregation is necessary. Often, sessions are unaware of what kinds of information would be helpful and have not developed a method or plan for data gathering. Some sessions have obtained information by conducting surveys but have failed to use the information in any significant way in the church's ministry.

Part I of this design assumes that it is important for every session to gather certain general information about the congregation. Three kinds will be considered: geographical location, unique characteristics and needs of persons, and talents and abilities of members.

Part II focuses on how persons are involved in the activities of the church.

Both sections will help participants understand the value of using data for more effective ministry.

Note: Because this design involves actual gathering of data about members of a local congregation, it is unsuitable for use in training events for more than one congregation.

Time Requirement: The time will depend on the size of the congregation and amount of data desired. Some of the work may be done before the study session.

GATHERING INFORMATION

Objectives

Participants will:
1. gather information about members of the congregation;
2. use the information in the congregation's ministry.

Preparation

1. Gather resources: congregational roll, telephone directory, city directory, large map of area (city/county).
2. Obtain supplies: index cards, pencils, colored-head straight pins.
3. Print or type names of members (active or inactive, children, youth and adults) of congregation on index cards, one name per card.
4. Duplicate resource sheet F-1 (Self Assessment Inventory) for use by Group III
5. For each workgroup, prepare a worksheet which summarizes the group's assigned task and contains space for reporting its findings.

Procedure

INTRODUCTION

Begin with a statement of the objective of the training. Then ask the participants, "How much do you know about the members of the congregation?" If general answers are offered, encourage them to be more specific. For example, ask if they know where specific individuals live or how many children are in the family. To further emphasize the need to be well-informed about persons in the congregation, use the following activity:

Activity

Place index cards, labeled with names of members of congregation, face down on the table. Ask participants to each choose a card. Ask them to write on the card all the general information they can about the person named. Such information should include where the person lives, marital status, children living at home, place of employment and leisure time interests. Participants should be cautioned not to discuss private information about the member. (5 minutes)

Ask each person to read aloud the name of the person on his/her card and share the information he/she has written. The profile should be read without comment or addition from the group because the purpose is to show by example how much or how little is known about members.

(If there are more than 10 or 12 participants, select only a few to read the profile they have written.)

Conclude by asking these questions:
1. Was more information known about some members than about other members?
2. Is it possible or even necessary for each elder to know general information about every church member?
3. If it is not possible, what is a practical method for obtaining such information when needed for ministry? (10 minutes)

DATA GATHERING

Divide the group into three workgroups. Each will be assigned a particular kind of data gathering.

Group I will gather geographical data. Group II will collect information concerning unique characteristics and needs of persons in the congregation. Group III will obtain information about talents and abilities of members.

It may not be possible to complete all the data gathering tasks at one meeting of the study group unless some of the work is assigned in advance. The questionnaire suggested for Group II especially requires extra time. The meeting time can then be spent analyzing the results of the questionnaire and preparing a report for the entire group.

Group I—Geographical Data

Using the congregational roll and a large area map, locate the homes of each church member. Most pastors maintain a roll which includes names and addresses of all persons connected to the congregation, both active and inactive as well as nonmembers who attend. If such a list is not available, the group could develop one while locating addresses on the map. A telephone directory and a city directory may be useful. As the addresses are located, they should be marked with colored pins, using different colors to indicate active, inactive and nonmembers. The location of the church should be marked in some extraordinary way.

The geographical information will be helpful in determining where the people live in relation to the church facility. For instance, do the majority live within a certain radius or are they scattered over a wide area? Awareness of geographical distribution is important in determining the ministry and outreach to the congregation and surrounding community. (The amount of time for this task depends on the size of the congregation and number of persons in the workgroup.)

Group II—Unique Characteristics and Needs

This group's work will depend on the specific characteristics and needs identified by the group as valuable. Three examples are suggested: persons in the congregation who have handicapped conditions (such as wheelchair bound), elderly persons who live alone, and invalids or shut-ins living at home or in nursing care homes. Other categories might include one-parent households, retired persons, and children whose parents do not attend church.

Using the congregational roll, the group should identify members with unique needs. An index card is prepared for each such person, listing the name, address and telephone number and noting the need.

The information can be helpful in identifying ways of caring for the congregation. For example, is there an individual who does not attend worship because the church building does not accommodate his/her handicapping condition? Or are there shut-ins who need regular visits from someone in addition to the pastor? (The amount of time for this analysis depends on the size of the congregation and number of persons in the workgroup.)

Group III—Talents and Abilities

Whether a congregation is large or small, persons within it have a variety of talents and abilities. Because part of the session's responsibility is to "initiate and coordinate the best measures for promoting and extending the work of the church" (*Constitution*, Section 4.5), it is helpful to develop some system for identifying the talents of members if they are to be involved effectively in accomplishing the church's ministry.

It is unlikely that elders will be able to compile this kind of information from studying the congregational roll. This kind of data is generally collected through some type of questionnaire. A sample is given on resource sheet F-1. It can be adapted by the workgroup according to the particular information being sought.

This information can be used by the session to match the abilities of the members of the congregation with the tasks and functions of the congregation. For example, if a person indicates on the questionnaire that he/she is interested in nursing home visitation, that person could be assigned to the committee that assists the pastor in visitation. Another example of the questionnaire's value could be identification of teachers and leaders for the church school.

The questionnaires need to be circulated in the congregation far enough in advance that they will be returned in time for the study session.

REPORTING OF WORKGROUPS

Reassemble the groups for reports. Someone from each workgroup should share its findings with the entire group, displaying maps, questionnaires and index cards and explaining pertinent information that has emerged. Each workgroup should also be prepared to suggest some ways the information can be used by the session for ministry.

USING DATA FOR EVALUATION

Objective

Using data about members of the congregation, participants will evaluate the involvement of persons in the opportunities available to them.

Preparation

1. Obtain supplies: newsprint sheets, masking tape, colored marking pens, index cards.
2. Write names of congregation members on index cards, one name per card.
3. Arrange for adequate table workspace for small groups and wall space for posting newsprint sheets.

Procedure

INTRODUCTION

Begin by explaining the objective, emphasizing that the study will give the session an overview of all the church activities and show how effectively the activities are meeting the needs of the congregation. (3 minutes)

IDENTIFY ACTIVITIES

Ask participants to identify the activities in which the members of the congregation are involved. As these are named, list them on a newsprint sheet. Make the list as inclusive as possible, naming activities which relate to every part of the church's life, such as worship, study, fellowship, recreation, etcetera. The items should be specific. For example, worship should be designated as morning and/or evening. (10 minutes)

The leader should then print each item at the top of a separate newsprint sheet. Attach these sheets with tape to the walls around the room so it will be convenient for participants to write on them. An additional sheet should be labeled "non-involvement."

DETERMINING INVOLVEMENT

Explain that the next step is to determine the involvement of each person of the congregation in the listed activities.

Activity

Divide the group into groups of two or three. Give each group an equal share of index cards containing names of congregation members.

Using the cards, the groups should describe involvement of each person in the church's activities. For example, the person may attend morning worship, sing in the choir and attend fellowship suppers. Another person may only be involved in Sunday evening youth meetings. Some notation should be made if the person has a leadership role in the activity named. If a person is not involved in any part of the church's program, it should be so noted on his/her card. (30 to 45 minutes)

The next task is for each small group to transfer the names to the appropriate newsprint sheets. The names should be color coded with marking pens to assist in the evaluation later. For example, use a green marker to write the person's name on the sheets if he/she is involved in two or more activities. Use another color if the person is involved in less than two activities. Use a red marker to list the person on the "non-involvement" sheet. If a person has a leadership position in an activity, the name should be circled. (30 to 45 minutes)

EVALUATE AND DISCUSS

With all participants together again, lists should be examined to answer such questions as
1. How many persons aren't involved in any activity?
2. What percentage are involved in two or more activities?
3. How many persons are in more than one leadership position? What does this say about the church's recruiting practices?

4. Are there activities which serve only a few members? Should these activities be re-evaluated for effectiveness?

5. What general picture emerges concerning the adequacy of the church's activities? (10 minutes)

SUMMARY AND CLOSING

If both parts of the design have been completed, the session will possess a fair amount of data. Participants should also understand that to minister effectively, certain information about the congregation is necessary.

It should be noted, however, that information can become obsolete quickly. Some decision should be reached for storing, maintaining and using the information. If the data collected is for a one-time project, it could be discarded when no longer needed. However, data such as that collected in the first part of the study can be continually helpful to the session if maintained accurately.

The study could be concluded with the reading of the "Fable of the File Folders" (resource sheet F-2), followed by a brief meditation or closing prayer. (5 minutes)

Bibliography

The Confession of Faith and Constitution of the Cumberland Presbyterian Church and Second Cumberland Presbyterian Church, 1984.

Recruiting and Utilizing the Abilities of Church Leaders, Unit 6, Continuing Education Series, The Geneva Press, 1975.

Caring for the Congregation

Focus

For church officers, the phrase "caring for the congregation" has a broader meaning than simply being concerned for certain individuals within the church. The *Confession of Faith* states that "officers have the responsibility to serve the church, to examine and receive members into the communion of the church, to care for and nurture them in the faith, and to discipline with love and justice those who offend the gospel and the laws of the church." (Church Government, Section 5.33) The *Constitution* states that the session "is charged with pastoral oversight" of the congregation. (Section 4.5)

This study focuses on three themes which explore the church officer's responsibility for congregational care: 1) communication between church officers and congregation, 2) assimilation of new members, and 3) pastoral care of the congregation.

Time Requirement: 2 to 2½ hours

Objectives

The participants will:

1. identify the existing channels of communication between the session/diaconate and the congregation;
2. determine the advantages or disadvantages of current communication channels and make plans for improvement;
3. analyze how candidates are prepared for church membership and received into the church;
4. describe the way in which new members are assimilated and suggest improvements;
5. identify scripture passages and statements in the *Confession of Faith and Constitution* which define responsibility of elders and deacons for pastoral care of the congregation;
6. suggest ways to improve the pastoral care plan.

Preparation

1. Gather resources: Bibles, *Confession of Faith.*
2. Obtain supplies: newsprint sheets, marking pens, pencils.
3. Print objectives on newsprint sheet.
4. Duplicate resource sheets G-1 (Situations), G-2 (New Member Enlistment), G-3 (What Some Churches Are Doing About New Members), G-4 (Rating Scale on Member Care).
5. Prepare lists of new members for each participant (see Enlistment and Assimilation of New Members, second activity).

Procedure

COMMUNICATION BETWEEN SESSION/DIACONATE AND CONGREGATION

Church officers may not recognize that good communication with the congregation is both a speaking and listening process. Introduce the subject with such questions as:

- How is important information about church programs and activities communicated to the congregation?
- How does the session become aware of problems within the congregation?
- Are ideas and views on issues solicited from the congregation?

Refer to the focus of the study and briefly review the first two objectives (written on newsprint). (5 minutes)

Activity

Ask participants to identify the existing channels of communication within the congregation, naming both written and verbal methods. As the responses are given, write them on a large newsprint sheet. Responses may include telephone calls, person to person, announcements from the pulpit, grapevine, newsletter, church bulletins, letters and others. Add any methods overlooked by the participants. (5 minutes)

Divide the group into two workgroups. Ask each to name a recorder and give him/her a newsprint sheet and marking pen. Ask one group to list the advantages of the communication methods; ask the other group to name the disadvantages. (10 minutes)

Reassemble the participants. Ask the recorders to share the results of the workgroups. As the results are presented, note on the original list of communication channels whether each method has more advantages or disadvantages.

Summarize by discussing the question, "How do our current communication methods affect how our church officers care for this congregation?" (5 minutes)

Activity

Divide the group into four workgroups. Give each one of the "situations" listed on resource sheet G-1. Ask each to develop a role play for the situation in two ways: the first would illustrate poor communication and the second would demonstrate good communication. (10 minutes)

Bring the groups together. Ask each to perform its "poor" and "good" versions, without indicating which is which. Ask the other participants why one role play represents better communication methods than the other. Encourage questions and discussion of the role plays. (20 minutes)

ENLISTMENT AND ASSIMILATION OF NEW MEMBERS

According to the *Constitution*, part of the pastoral oversight responsibility of the session is to receive new members into the church. (Section 4.5b) The *Constitution* also states that a church member is under the jurisdiction of the session of the particular church to which he/she belongs. (Section 2.21) This means that the session's responsibility for member care extends beyond simply receiving the member into the church.

Introduce this part of the study by calling attention to the third and fourth objectives. The following activity will help participants identify how candidates are now being prepared for and received into church membership. (5 minutes)

Activity

Give resource sheets G-2 and G-3 to each participant. Ask them to individually read the sheets, then pair with another participant to discuss and complete sheet G-2. (10 minutes)

Continue the discussion with the entire group, focusing on these questions:
* Are we adequately fulfilling our responsibility as church officers in the matter of new member enlistment?
* In what ways can we improve enlistment of new members?
* Are there more methods listed that our congregation might consider doing? (5 minutes)

Activity

In this activity, participants will determine how well they support and encouragement involvement of new members during the first few months of their membership.

Give each participant a list of the new members received into the church in the past year. Ask participants to individually answer the following questions about each person on the list:
* Is the person still a member?
* Is the person active in the church? Be as specific as possible, describing the person's extent of involvement in various aspects of the church program.
(Time needed will depend on number of new members studied.)

As a group, share information about the persons on the list until each person's involvement in the church is fully described.

Summarize by asking these questions:
* Is anyone on the list not involved in any church programs?
* Are we meeting our responsibility as church officers in bringing new members into the church program?
* How can we improve assimilation of new members? (10 minutes)

Note: Church sessions may wish to pursue the last questions of both activities by developing specific plans of action, referring to resource sheet G-3 for suggestions.

PASTORAL CARE OF THE CONGREGATION

Church officers may tend to think that pastoral care of the congregation is solely the responsibility of the minister in charge. As noted in the focus for this study, the *Confession of Faith* makes clear that church officers must also consider this caring and nurturing of members as part of their responsibility.

In his book, *The Pastoral Ministry of Church Officers,* Charlie W. Shedd asks these questions: "How well have we pushed down the partition between the session room and the homes of our parish? Do we knock on enough doors? Do we cross enough thresholds? Do our members know their leaders care not only about the church but about the inner personal needs in individual souls?"

Introduce this part of the study by reviewing the fifth and sixth objectives. These activities will help participants become more aware of their role in the pastoral care of members. (5 minutes)

Activity

Divide the group into workgroups of three or four. Assign each group one of these Scripture passages:

Matthew 18:15-20	John 21:15-17
I Thess. 5:12-15	James 5:14-16
Titus 1:5-9	Romans 15:1-6
I Peter 5:1-4	Acts 20:28-31

Ask each group to respond to the question, "How does this passage instruct the church officer in the matter of caring for church members?" (10 minutes)

Reassemble the entire group. Ask someone from each workgroup to read its assigned scripture and share the group's response to the question.

Activity

Give resource sheet G-4 to each participant. Clarify the directions, then ask each person to complete the sheet. (5 minutes)

As a group, discuss the results of the individual ratings, noting points of agreement or disagreement. (10 minutes)

Activity

Based on the discussion in the previous activity, enter into "brain-storming" to generate ideas for improving the present approach to pastoral care by church officers. As suggestions are made, write them on a large newsprint sheet. All ideas are to be accepted and written without comment or evaluation. These suggestions may be added to the list:

* Organize the congregation into zones or districts with persons assigned to keep in touch with members in his/her area.
* Set up a telephone network to keep in touch with members, particularly older persons and shut-ins.
* Set up a pastoral care committee or committees, chaired by church officers.
* Keep a record of attendance and participation of each family in the congregation.

(Designate a definite length of time for the brainstorming.)

When the brainstorming is completed, evaluate the suggestions on the following basis:

1. Select the ideas best suited for implementation by your group of officers.
2. Rate those ideas in order of importance (ask each person to list first, second and third choices, then tally choices of entire group).
3. Decide how the selected suggestions will be implemented. (10 minutes)

CLOSING

Bibliography

Communication, Continuing Education Series, Unit 5, John Knox Press, 1975.

Caring for Church Members, Continuing Education Series, Unit 7, John Knox Press, 1976.

The Pastoral Ministry of Church Officers, Charlie W. Shedd, John Knox Press, 1976.

The Noble Task, the Elder, Andrew A. Jumper, John Knox Press, Atlanta, GA, 1965.

Planning the Work of the Church

Focus

Planning the work of the church requires a clear understanding of the mission of the church and how the mission directs what is done through the church's programs and activities. The *Confession of Faith* defines this mission in terms of being nurtured and sustained by worship, proclamation, study of the word, celebration of the sacraments and by witnessing to all persons who have not received Christ as Lord and Savior. (*Confession of Faith,* Section 5.28)

Each congregation is called to carry out the mission of the church through the specific areas of ministry as organized and directed by the church officers.

This study gives church officers a better understanding of the mission of the church as it relates to the church's ministry.

Time Requirement: 2 to 2½ hours

Objectives

The participants will:
1. define the mission of the church;
2. identify and evaluate the areas of ministry through which the mission is being accomplished;
3. state goals and develop plans for fulfilling the mission through various facets of the church's ministry.

Preparation

1. Gather resources: Bibles, *Confession of Faith.*
2. Obtain supplies: newsprint sheets, masking tape, marking pen, paper, pencils, index cards.
3. Print objectives on newsprint sheet.
4. Duplicate resource sheets H-1 (Defining the Mission of the Church), H-2 (Areas of the Church's Ministry) and H-3 (Planning Guide).

Procedure

INTRODUCTION

Refer to the focus of the study and review the objectives (written on newsprint and displayed to the participants). Allow time for questions and clarification of the objectives. (5 minutes)

Activity

Give each participant a sheet of paper and pencil. Ask each to write the phrase, "mission of the church," at the top of his/her sheet. Using the upper half of the sheet, participants are to quickly write all the words that come to mind when they hear the phrase, "mission of the church." (2 minutes)

On the lower half of the sheet, they are to list what goes on in their church during a week. For instance, the list would probably include worship services, church school, choir practice, etcetera. (5 minutes)

Ask for a volunteer to write his/her "mission of the church" words on newsprint. Encourage the other participants to suggest different words from their lists. Ask a different volunteer to write his/her list of church activities on a separate newsprint sheet. Again, allow additions from the group.

Post the completed lists on the wall for easy viewing. Do not pursue a group discussion of the lists at this time. (5 to 10 minutes)

DEFINING MISSION OF THE CHURCH

The introductory activity should reveal that a definition of the church's mission varies according to individual interpretation. In the following activity, participants discuss, in small groups, their understanding of the mission of the church in terms of biblical and confessional statements and other theological writings.

Activity

Divide the group into workgroups of three persons. Give each person resource sheet H-1. Using the sheet as a study guide, ask each group to 1) write a definition of the mission of the church in light of the information on the sheet, and 2) discuss the relevancy of this definition to the church's activities that were named in the preceding activity. (15 minutes)

Reassemble the entire group. Ask a volunteer from one or two workgroups to share definitions of the church's mission and its implication for the activities of the church. Allow questions and additional comments from other small groups. (5 minutes)

EVALUATING PRESENT AREAS OF MINISTRY

The activities listed by the group in the introductory activity will generally fall into these areas of ministry: worship and celebration, education, evangelism, stewardship, outreach, member care, building and grounds, leadership and administration, and fellowship. Other areas may also be listed.

Activity

Give each participant a pencil and resource sheet H-2. Ask each to read the categories and then assign the activities listed in the introductory activity to the appropriate categories. This will provide a general evaluation of where most activities are centered.

Then ask each participant to choose four areas of ministry which, in his/her opinion, need the most attention and extra effort in the near future. Each person should number the areas in order of importance, 1, 2, 3 or 4, with 1 indicating the most important and 4 the least important. (5 minutes)

Note: These choices do not need to reflect the overview revealed in the first activity. Each person should follow his/her own feelings in ranking the areas.

Divide a newsprint sheet into sections similar to resource sheet H-2; label the sections. Use the sections to tally the participants' choices of the areas they believe need extra attention.

To tally, assign a numerical value to each rank: each first choice is worth 4 points, second choice worth 3 points, third choice worth 2 points and fourth choice worth 1 point. For example, ask, "In the WORSHIP/CELEBRATION category, please raise your hand if you gave it first priority." Record the number of persons × 4 points. Then ask, "How many feel this was a second priority?" and record that number of persons × 3, etcetera. Repeat with remaining categories.

Ask for volunteers to explain their choices. It will be helpful to have someone note on another newsprint sheet significant information pertaining to each area. For example, a participant identifying STEWARDSHIP as a first choice may suggest a need for conducting an every member canvas; the need for an every member canvas would be noted on the second newsprint sheet.

When all choices have been reported, add the numbers in each chart section. The totals should give a general indication of areas of concern. (20 minutes)

STATING GOALS AND DEVELOPING PLANS

Using the four areas of greatest concern, participants should now focus on developing some specific plans for those areas.

Activity

Set up four workgroups, one for each area of concern. If possible allow individuals to choose the area most closely related to his/her interests or abilities. Distribute resource sheet H-3 to each group. Briefly explain that it provides a step by step approach to planning.

Ask each group to discuss the needs expressed in its assigned area and then write a goal which addresses the needs. Each group may also wish to develop objectives and outline strategies to be used in accomplishing the goal. (45 minutes)

Reassemble the entire group and ask each workgroup to share its work. Encourage participants to identify the place (committee, group, individual, etcetera) through which the goals would be most effectively implemented. (10 minutes)

CLOSING

Use the following thoughts and scripture to remind the participants that no planned activity or program in the church should become an end unto itself. At every point in planning the work of the congregation, the question must be asked: "Will this activity help fulfill the mission of the church?"

The words of Jesus in John 15:4 are a reminder of how the mission is to be accomplished: "Remain united to me, and I will remain united to you. A branch cannot bear fruit by itself; it can do so only if it remains in the vine. In the same way you cannot bear fruit unless you remain in me." (TEV) (3 minutes)

EVALUATION

Give each participant an index card and pencil. Ask each to write the letters A, B and C at the top of the card. Call attention to the three objectives for this study (on newsprint). Ask participants to indicate, with a "yes" or "no" under A, B and C on their card, whether they believe each objective had been met. Encourage them to write comments explaining any or all of their responses. (5 minutes)

Bibliography

Planning a Church Officer Retreat, by Edwin W. Albright and Mary Baine Rudolph, Presbyterian Church in the U.S., 1981.

Using Planning to Improve Decision Making, Continuing Education Series, Unit 13, John Knox Press, 1978.

Judicatories

Focus

In the *Confession of Faith* the Preamble to the *Constitution* states "although no detailed form of church government is laid down in scripture, the connectional nature of the church is clearly affirmed. The Presbyterian form embodies the connectional nature of the church in a manner compatible with scripture."

It further explains that a representative form of government was used by the synagogue with elders acting in behalf of people in matters relating to the life of the synagogue. The name Presbyterian derives from the Greek word "presbuteros" that is translated elder. An assembly of elders is a presbuterion (presbytery).

When elders and deacons are ordained in the Cumberland Presbyterian Church/Second Cumberland Presbyterian Church, they are asked to approve and uphold the government of the church. Elders are also asked to promise to share in a responsible way in the decisions made in the various judicatories or levels of church government.

In this study, church officers examine the connectional structure of the Presbyterian system of church government so they can better fulfill their responsibility.

Time Requirement: 1 hour

Objectives

Participants will:
1. name the various levels of church government in the Presbyterian system;
2. identify the interrelated functions of each church court as outlined in the Constitution;
3. examine the function of elders as representatives to higher church courts;
4. identify the resources available to local church officers from higher levels of church government.

Preparation

1. Gather resources: *Confession of Faith*, copies of presbyterial, synodical and General Assembly minutes.
2. Obtain supplies: newsprint sheets, masking tape, marking pens, pencils, paper.
3. Print objectives on large newsprint sheet.
4. Duplicate resource sheets I-1 (Flow Chart), I-2 (Functions of Judicatories), I-3 (Interrelated Functions of Judicatories), I-4 (Serving as Representatives to Higher Judicatories) and I-5 (Organizational Structure of Judicatories).
5. Print discussion items from Higher Judicatories as Sources of Information/Aid on newsprint sheet.

Procedure

INTRODUCTION

Introduce the study by referring briefly to the information in the focus and reviewing the objectives (on newsprint sheet). Allow questions and clarify any of the objectives. (5 minutes)

LEVELS OF CHURCH GOVERNMENT

On a chalkboard or large newsprint sheet, list the following: Session, Presbytery, Synod and General Assembly. Explain that these are the names given to the levels of Cumberland Presbyterian Church government.

Activity

Give each participant a pencil and sheet of paper. Ask each to sketch a diagram of how he/she perceives the structure of the church, labeling the diagram with the names of the various levels of government. Explain that the levels should be connected with lines to show the "flow" of responsibility between levels. For example, in a school system, the superintendent might be at the top; below him/her, the principal; below him/her, the teachers, and then the students below the teachers. (5 minutes)

Give each participant resource sheet I-1 (or reproduce the chart on a large newsprint sheet). Ask each to compare his/her diagram with the one on the resource sheet. Note that even though the sketches may vary, two factors should be similar: there are four levels of church courts, each with a unique role, and these four judicatories are interrelated and all a part of the presbyterian form of church government. (5 minutes)

INTERRELATED FUNCTIONS OF JUDICATORIES

Building on the flow chart which shows the connectional system of courts, participants will now explore the interrelated functions of the various levels.

Activity

Give each participant resource sheet I-2 to use as guide sheet for completing resource sheet I-3. Divide the group into four workgroups. Give each group one resource sheet I-3. It contains a dozen actions/situations which involve two or more church courts. Direct the groups to analyze each situation and then list the courts that would usually be involved. For example, the two judicatories directly involved in calling a pastor for a congregation are the session and the presbytery. (10 minutes)

Reassemble the participants to compare and discuss their conclusions. Emphasize that the actions/situations listed are only a sample of how the judicatories interrelate. (10 minutes)

SERVING AS REPRESENTATIVES TO HIGHER COURTS

Elders are sometimes reluctant to serve as representatives to higher judicatories because they are uncertain about what is expected of them. The reluctance contributes to the practice of continually sending the same persons as representatives to the higher courts.

Use the following activity to help session members learn the duties of delegates to presbytery and synod and commissioners to the General Assembly.

Activity

Give each participant resource sheet I-4. Ask each to study the information, noting any specific items which need clarification. (5 minutes)

Lead a group discussion on each category of the resource sheet, calling for questions noted by individuals during the study time. Discuss any additional questions not answered on the resource sheet. Explain the relationship of the pastor to the higher judicatories and how it differs from that of ruling elders. (15 minutes)

HIGHER JUDICATORIES AS SOURCES OF INFORMATION/AID

The presbytery, synod and General Assembly can provide valuable assistance and information to local congregations through systems of committees, boards and agencies. Church officers should become familiar with this system so they may use the resources or be called on to serve as a member of a committee, board or agency of a higher judicatory.

Resource sheet I-5 gives examples of the organizational structures of a presbytery, synod and the General Assembly. Use this sheet (adapted for accuracy in your particular presbytery and synod) to describe the type of help available. Listed below are four examples (written on newsprint) to illustrate the resources.

- The local Christian Education Committee wants to examine resource materials and train officers for vacation church school. Sources: presbytery Christian Education Committee and/or denominational Board of Christian Education.
- The CPW wants to support a mission project. Sources: mission boards and committees on every higher judicatorial level.
- A session needs to secure a pastor. Sources: denominational Board of Missions' Department of Professional Services, presbytery and/or synod mission agencies.
- A youth group has several members interested in attending summer camps. Sources: Christian Education boards/committees on every higher judicatorial level.

Encourage participants to express other needs or concerns which can then be used to illustrate how the judicatorial system can respond to local needs. Emphasize the responsibility shared by each level for making the system function effectively. (10 minutes)

CLOSING AND EVALUATION

The following quote is suggested for use in closing the study:

". . . a responsibility that is among the most important is often given the least attention: to appoint a ruling elder commissioner to attend each meeting of presbytery and to encourage this delegate to participate fully in the work and deliberations of the presbytery and to report back.

"This one responsibility carries importance of tremendous significance to the whole concept of Presbyterianism. It means, in brief, at least four vital things:

"1. The session is a key to all that happens in the church—not only in the congregation but in the presbytery, synod and General Assembly.

"2. Every ruling elder serving on a session has both an opportunity and a responsibility to be involved either directly or indirectly in this beyond-the-congregation action.

"3. Each commissioner to a higher court has a responsibility to be an effective communication link between that court and the congregation.

"4. The system simply won't work if these opportunities and responsibilities are shirked."

(From *Help and How To Get It*, Unit 2, Continuing Education Series, Church Officer Development, John Knox Press, 1975, p. 21)

Evaluate by asking participants to describe how they will use the new information from the study in their service as church officers. (10 minutes)

Bibliography

The Confession of Faith and Government of the Cumberland Presbyterian Church and Second Cumberland Presbyterian Church, 1984.

Church Officer Pre-Ordination Curriculum, Unit IV, Church Order, The Geneva Press, 1975.

Help and How To Get It, Unit 2, Continuing Education Series, Church Officer Development, John Knox Press, 1975.

Dealing With Conflict

Focus

Included in the statements in the *Constitution* concerning qualifications of both elders and deacons are the words "wisdom," "maturity of judgment" and "discretion." These terms indicate ways in which church officers exemplify the gospel. One question asked of candidates for the office of elder or deacon is, "Do you promise to promote the peace, unity and purity of the church?" (*Constitution*, Section 2.92)

Indeed, elders and deacons are often called upon to resolve conflict which arises within the congregation. It is important that church officers develop leadership skills which will enable them to deal effectively and creatively with conflict.

In this study, participants will study effective ways of conflict resolution.

Time Requirement: 1 to 1½ hours

Objectives

At the end of the study, participants will:

1. understand the wisdom of dealing openly with conflict situations;
2. be able to identify potential sources of conflict and characteristics which surround conflict;
3. understand some principles to use in resolving conflict.

Preparation

1. Gather resources: Bibles, *Confession of Faith*.
2. Obtain supplies: newsprint sheets, marking pen, masking tape, index cards, pencils.
3. Duplicate resource sheet J-1 (Dealing with Conflict).
4. Write questions for first activity on large newsprint sheet.

Procedure

INTRODUCTION

Make introductions as necessary to assure that all members of the group are acquainted, creating a congenial environment. Review the objectives, revising or expanding as suggested by the group. (5 minutes)

Begin with the question, "Why should we study conflict management?" Encourage participants to suggest answers. As answers are suggested, write them on chalkboard or large newsprint sheet.

Give each person resource sheet J-1; ask each to silently read the material under the heading, "Why Deal with Conflict at All?" Following the reading, ask participants to look again at the responses they gave earlier to "Why should we study conflict management?" Are there changes or additions which should now be made in response to the question?

In summarizing, emphasize that suppressing conflict can lead to division which is destructive. On the other hand, dealing openly with conflict can lead to reconciliation. (10 minutes)

IDENTIFYING POTENTIAL CONFLICT

It sometimes seems that disagreements within the church are more intense and difficult to resolve than other conflict situations. In order to deal quickly and effectively with conflict, church leaders should be able to identify potential problems and have some understanding of characteristics that may surround the conflict.

The following activities deal with conflict identification. The first activity is suggested for use in groups with participants from more than one church; the second activity is suggested for participants from a single church.

Activity

Give each person an index card and pencil. Ask each to list one or two conflict situations they recall in church. Emphasize that persons are not to be identified by name; refer to them as "between Sunday school teachers" or "between youth and adults," etcetera.

Ask each participant to team with another person to describe and discuss characteristics of the situations each has recorded. Again, emphasize that persons actually involved in the incidents not be identified. Use the other side of the index cards to record information from the sharing. In their discussions, encourage the pairs to answer questions such as

* What was the issue?

- Was the apparent issue the "real" problem?
- What was the relationship of the individuals?
- Were there obvious differences in the values of the persons?
- Were all parties seeking resolution of the conflict?
- Did persons reveal concerns or needs which were contributing factors to the issue? (15 minutes)

Reassemble the participants. Ask for one or two volunteers to share information from the discussion done in pairs. In answering the guide questions, what was discovered that helped characterize the conflict situations?

Use the following quote to summarize:

"The basic issue in a conflict can usually be seen by looking beyond the 'problem' itself to what is going on in the relationship of those involved. Often conflict arises because one person or a group does not recognize or understand the values of the other."

(From *Dealing Creatively with Conflict*, Unit 3, Continuing Education Series, The Geneva Press, 1975, p. 9)

Activity

Using brainstorming, ask participants to describe several potential conflict situations in a typical congregation. As these are named, list them on newsprint. Situations might include:

- Disagreement among teachers about church school literature
- Problem with misuse of church's audiovisual and sound equipment
- Dissatisfaction over leadership and activities of youth
- Disagreement over use of church building by outside groups
- Adversarial relationship between session and diaconate
- Members of congregation unhappy with change in order of worship

Refer to resource sheet J-1 and ask each participant to read the material under the heading "How Do We Handle Conflict?" (5 minutes)

Divide the group into workgroups of three to five persons. Ask each group to choose one of the potential conflict situations (listed on the newsprint sheet). Instruct each group to develop a two-part role play that will illustrate the conflict being dealt with competitively and integratively. Refer them to the basic principles in "How Do We Handle Conflict?" for direction in developing the role plays. (10 minutes)

Reassemble the participants for presentation of the role plays. Allow questions and encourage discussion following each presentation. (15 minutes)

CLOSING AND EVALUATION

Refer again to the question asked of church officer candidates: "Do you promise to promote the peace, unity and purity of the church?" Follow this reference with a reading of Philippians 2:1-11. Though conflict may not always be avoidable, church officers can effectively manage such situations.

Give each person an index card and pencil. Ask each to complete this sentence: "In respect to conflict management, today I learned _____." (5 minutes)

Bibliography

The Confession of Faith and Government of the Cumberland Presbyterian Church and Second Cumberland Presbyterian Church, 1984.

Dealing Creatively with Conflict, Unit 3, Continuing Education Series, Church Officer Development, The Geneva Press, 1975.

Leadership and Conflict, Speed B. Leas, Creative Leadership Series, Abingdon Press, Nashville, 1982.

Resource Sheet A-1

PLANS FOR FULFILLING THE DUTIES OF MY OFFICE (Elder)

My Duties as an Elder	*My Priorities*	*How I Will Carry Out This Duty*
1. To represent the people in government and leadership of the church	1 2 3	
2. To be particularly attentive to persons who have not confessed Jesus Christ as Lord and Savior, those who are spiritually weak and those who need to be instructed in the faith.	1 2 3	
3. To visit the people in their homes, praying with and for them, especially for the sick, those who mourn, and others in need.	1 2 3	
4. To encourage people to share in the worship, study, witness and service of the church through a faithful stewardship of their time, talents and money.	1 2 3	
5. To inform the pastor of any concerns that need attention.	1 2 3	
6. To witness to the gospel as a leader of the congregation by exemplifying good character, sound faith, wisdom, maturity of judgment, discretion, conversation, knowledge of the doctrine and government of the church, and competency to perform the duties of the office.	1 2 3	
7. To engage in study and preparation as are appropriate to the office in order to better perform my duties.	1 2 3	

PLANS FOR FULFILLING THE DUTIES OF MY OFFICE (Deacon)

My Duties as a Deacon	My Priorities	How I Will Carry Out This Duty
1. To lead and coordinate activities of persons, committees and groups in ministering to the poor, the elderly, the sick, orphans, refugees, prisoners and others in distress.	1 2 3	
2. To make periodic reports to the session.	1 2 3	
3. To formulate budgets and assume other financial responsibilities as requested by the session.	1 2 3	
4. To witness to the gospel as a leader of the congregation by exemplifying sound judgment, good character, compassion for those in need, availability to people and a deep abiding faith in Jesus Christ, whose example in ministry I follow.	1 2 3	
5. To engage in study and preparation as are appropriate to the office in order to better perform my duties.	1 2 3	

PRAYER/LITANY

Leader: O God, you have called us to be like salt for all humankind. You have said we are to be like light for the whole world.

Response: WE HAVE FAITH, HOLY GOD, BUT NOT ENOUGH.

Leader: You have told us to love our enemies and pray for those who persecute us.

Response: WE HAVE FAITH, HOLY GOD, BUT NOT ENOUGH.

Leader: You have told us not to store up riches here on earth, that we can't be loyal to two masters.

Response: WE HAVE FAITH, HOLY GOD, BUT NOT ENOUGH.

Leader: You have said not to judge others because there may be a "log in our own eye."

Response: WE HAVE FAITH, HOLY GOD, BUT NOT ENOUGH.

Leader: "Do for others what you want them to do for you," is your rule we call golden.

Response: WE HAVE FAITH, HOLY GOD, BUT NOT ENOUGH.

Leader: Your words and your example continually challenge us.

Response: WE HAVE FAITH, HOLY GOD, BUT NOT ENOUGH. HELP US HAVE MORE. AMEN.

Resource Sheet B-2

MY FAITH JOURNEY

Use this chart to think about your journey through life. At each stage try to recall your faith experience, specifically in relation to understandings about God, Jesus Christ, the Bible and the church. Write a brief description of experiences that were important in your journey.

Early Childhood   Elementary Years

Youth   Adulthood

(Adapted from Appendix C1, Team Building, Design C, Planning a Church Officer Retreat, Edwin W. Albright Jr. and Mary Baine Rudolph, General Assembly Mission Board, Presbyterian Church in the U.S., 1981. Used with permission.)

SUGGESTIONS FOR DEVELOPING DEVOTIONAL MODELS

Scripture

—Choose scripture which has a particular personal meaning and explain this special meaning to the group.

—Choose a passage which has relevance for a specific occasion, such as Ephesians 4 which emphasizes the unity of believers.

—Use a passage which can be read as dialogue, such as portions of John 4 (Jesus and the Samaritan woman) or John 11 (raising Lazarus from death).

Prayer

—Write a prayer-litany which can be used by the group (see resource sheet B-1).

—Use selected parts of prayers from the Scriptures such as Psalm 51:10-13 or Psalm 25:4-7.

—Ask the group members to pray silently, directing their thoughts with statements appropriate to the occasion.

Music and Devotional Thoughts

—Read words of a hymn for an effective devotional thought, such as verses from "We Are One in the Spirit."

—Use a cassette tape of a hymn or spiritual song in lieu of actual singing by the group or to aid with group singing.

—Use books of meditations or daily devotional guides such as *These Days* for short inspirational thoughts.

Resource Sheet C-1

IS THIS OUR RESPONSIBILITY?

Match the situations described in the left column with the statements of responsibility in the right column.

_____ 1. The church school, the children's choir, and the Scouts, each involving many of the same children, have each announced a major event for the same day.

_____ 2. A notice has come from presbytery that the congregation has not had a ruling elder delegate at presbytery meeting during the last year.

_____ 3. It is common knowledge that a disgruntled member of the congregation has been misquoting the pastor and others in the congregation to the detriment of the church.

_____ 4. Giving to missions has declined.

_____ 5. A new class of elders and deacons has just been elected at the congregational meeting.

_____ 6. A young child's parents, both active members of the church, say they do not want their child baptized until he is old enough to make his confession of faith.

_____ 7. An appeal for contributions to a flood relief fund is being made by a community group. Several church members think an offering should be taken in next week's service of worship.

_____ 8. The session has asked every group in the church to present a statement of goals and proposed program for the coming year at a congregational planning meeting.

_____ 9. A request for their church letters has come to the church from a family who has been transferred to another town.

_____ 10. A notice has come from the clerk of the presbytery that it is time to review the church session record.

a. To elect representatives to the higher judicatories.

b. To grant letters of dismission.

c. To urge upon parents the importance of presenting their children for baptism.

d. To initiate and coordinate the best measures for promoting the work of the church.

e. To encourage the stewardship of church members.

f. To keep an accurate record of proceedings to submit to presbytery annually for review.

g. To resolve questions of doctrine and discipline.

h. To ordain and install elders and deacons.

i. To establish and give oversight to church schools, Bible classes, fellowship and other organizations within the church.

j. To order and supervise collections for godly purposes and oversee the finances of the church.

(Duties of session listed taken from Confession of Faith and Constitution*)*

Adapted from Form 1-A, Work of the Session and the Diaconate, *Continuing Education Series, The Geneva Press, 1975. Used with permission.*

Resource Sheet C-2

SAMPLE ITEMS FROM SESSION MINUTES

1. A letter of transfer was granted to a church member.

2. The pastor and clerk were asked to study and revise the roll of inactive church members.

3. Youth Director's report was heard and approved.

4. Treasurer's report was reviewed and approved.

5. A committee was appointed to develop guidelines for use of new church van.

6. The report of the Worship Committee about holding special Lenten services was heard.

7. Nominees for new elders were approved.

8. Delegate to presbytery was elected.

9. Approval was given for youth to collect money for UNICEF.

10. The report of the Christian Education Committee was heard and names were approved for church school teachers and leaders.

11. Approval was given for use of church building by a community agency.

12. A report from Christian Education concerning formation of a new church school class was heard.

13. Pastor's monthly report was heard and approved.

14. Report of the Building and Grounds Committee concerning maintenance of property was heard.

15. Action was taken to receive new church members.

16. A report from the Missions Committee concerning inviting a missionary to speak at the church was heard.

CORPORATE RESPONSIBILITIES OF THE SESSION

(Organized into four major categories and taken from the *Confession of Faith and Constitution*.)

I. WORSHIP AND SACRAMENTS

—Lead the members in public worship, including praying, singing of praises, reading the Scriptures, presenting tithes and offerings, preaching the word, and celebrating the sacraments.

—Assemble the congregation and provide for worship when there is no minister.

II. ADMINISTRATIVE

—Call a pastor, subject to approval of presbytery.

—Receive members into the church.

—Grant letters of dismission, which when given for parents shall always include names of baptized children.

—Ordain and install elders and deacons when elected and require these officers to devote themselves to their responsibilities.

—Examine the proceedings and supervise the work of the deacons.

—Order and supervise collections for godly purposes, and, in general, oversee the finances of the church and the care and use of properties of the church.

—Elect representatives to the higher judicatories and require a report of their diligence and the decisions of the judicatory.

—Observe and carry out the injunctions of the higher judicatories.

—Hold title to the property of the church and execute all transactions required by civil law.

—Keep an accurate record of proceedings which must be submitted to presbytery for review.

—Keep a record of congregational meetings, marriages, baptisms, additions, and the death and dismission of church members.

III. JUDICIAL AND DISCIPLINARY

—Resolve questions of doctrine and discipline in the congregation.

—Admonish or suspend members found guilty in a disciplinary hearing, subject to appeal to presbytery.

IV. MOTIVATIONAL AND EDUCATIONAL

—Lead members in personal witness to unbelievers and those out of fellowship with the church.

—Assist in pastoral care of families.

—Urge parents to present their children for baptism.

—Establish and give oversight to church schools, Bible classes, fellowship and other organizations within the church, giving special attention to nurture of children.

—Initiate and coordinate the best measures for promoting and extending the work of the church.

—Encourage the stewardship of church members.

—Lead members in activities of fellowship appropriate to the family of God.

CORPORATE RESPONSIBILITIES OF THE DIACONATE

(The primary source for the areas of responsibility for the diaconate is found in the *Constitution,* Sections 2.80-2.84.)

Deacons are elected and ordained to:

1. Lead the church in its care of the poor and others in need, administering the funds provided by the church for these purposes.

2. Lead and coordinate activities of persons, committees and groups in ministering to the poor, the elderly, the sick, orphans, refugees, prisoners, and others in distress.

3. Make periodic reports to the session.

4. Formulate budgets and assume other financial responsibilities (*if the session has delegated this responsibility to the diaconate.*)

BROKEN SQUARES (Directions)

A "set" consists of five envelopes containing pieces of cardboard which have been cut into different shapes and which, when properly arranged will form five squares of equal size. One "set" is needed for each group of five persons.

To prepare a "set," cut five cardboard squares of equal size. The accompanying patterns are based on five-inch squares. Transfer the markings of the pattern to the squares, lightly pencilling the lower case letters so they may be later erased. Cut along the indicated lines. Pieces with the same letter should be the same size.

Several combinations of pieces will enable players to form one or two squares but only one combination will permit formation of five 5×5-inch squares.

Mark five envelopes A, B, C, D and E. Assign the cardboard pieces to the five envelopes as follows:

Envelope A contains pieces i, h, e
       B contains pieces a, a, a, c
       C contains pieces a, j
       D contains pieces d, f
       E contains pieces g, b, f, c

As you place the pieces in each envelope, erase the pencilled lower case letter from each piece; write on each its envelope letter. This will make it easy to return the pieces to the proper envelope after a group has completed the game.

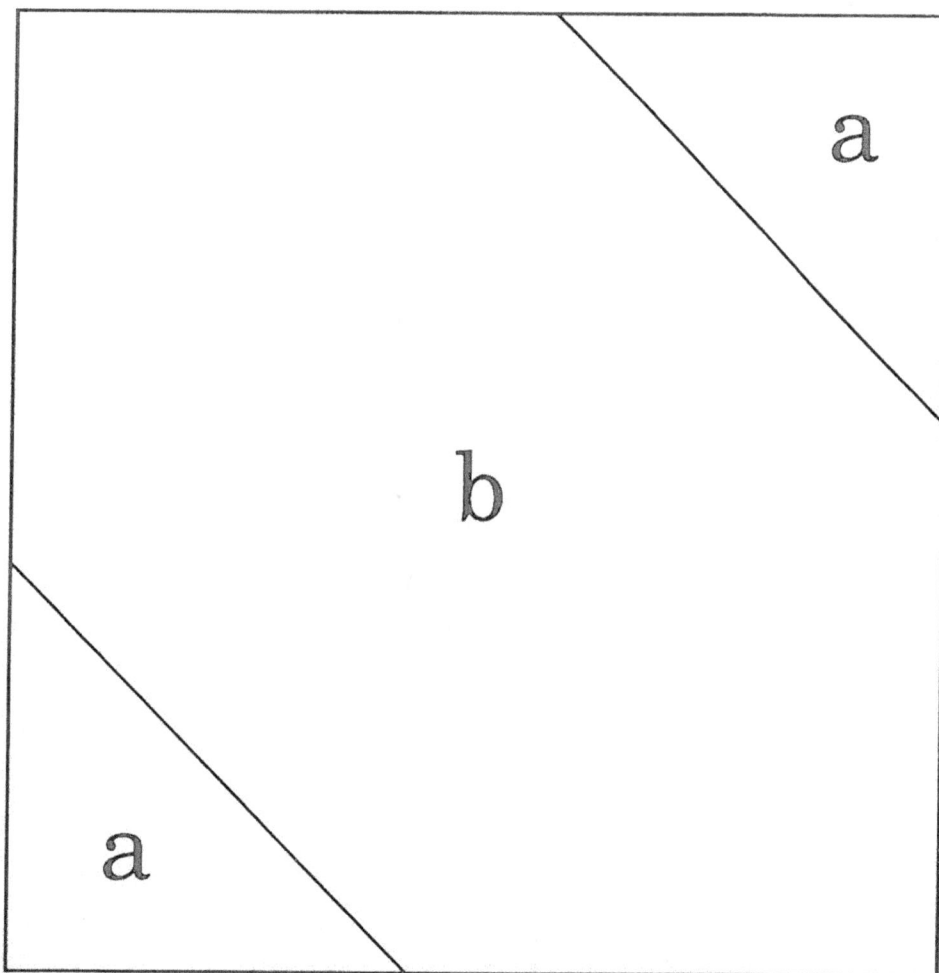

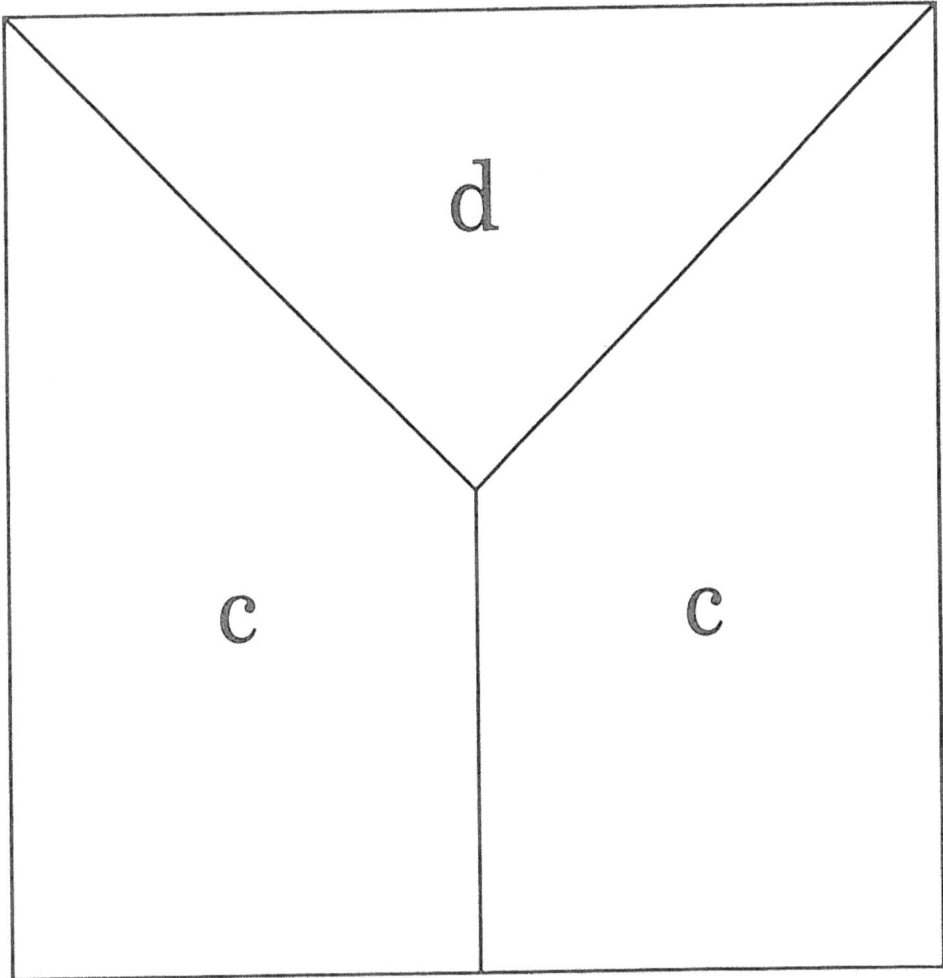

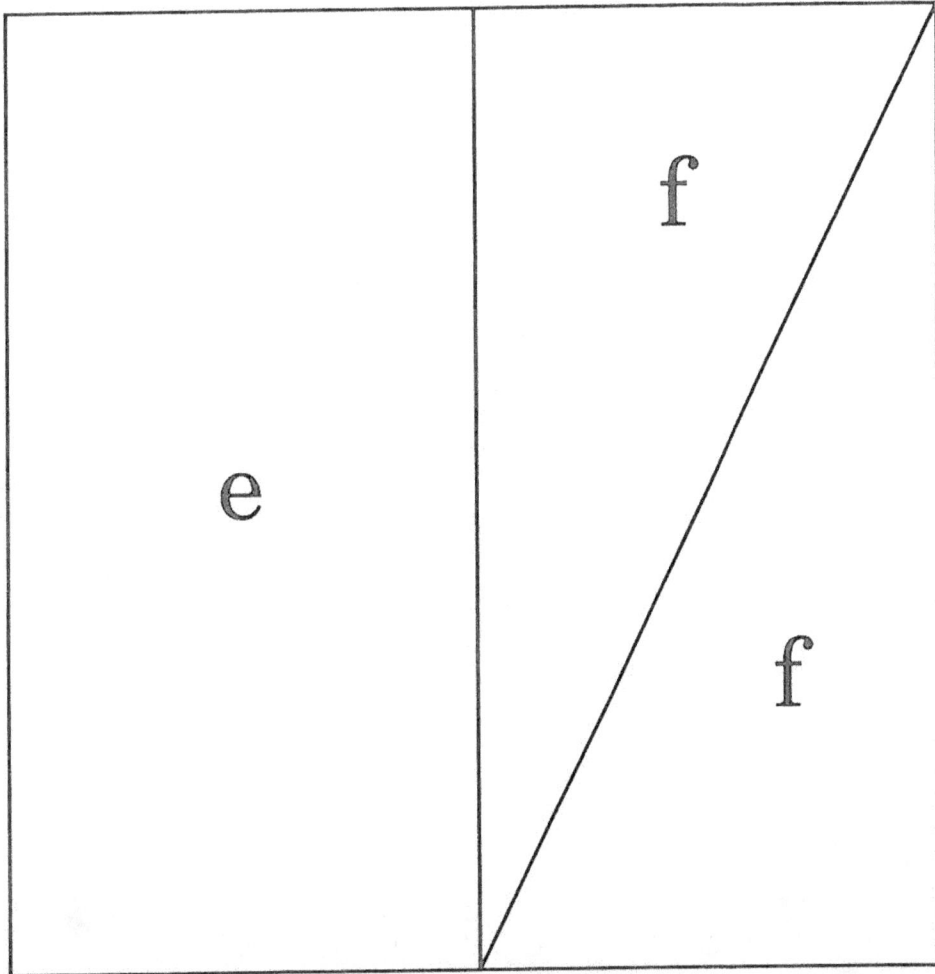

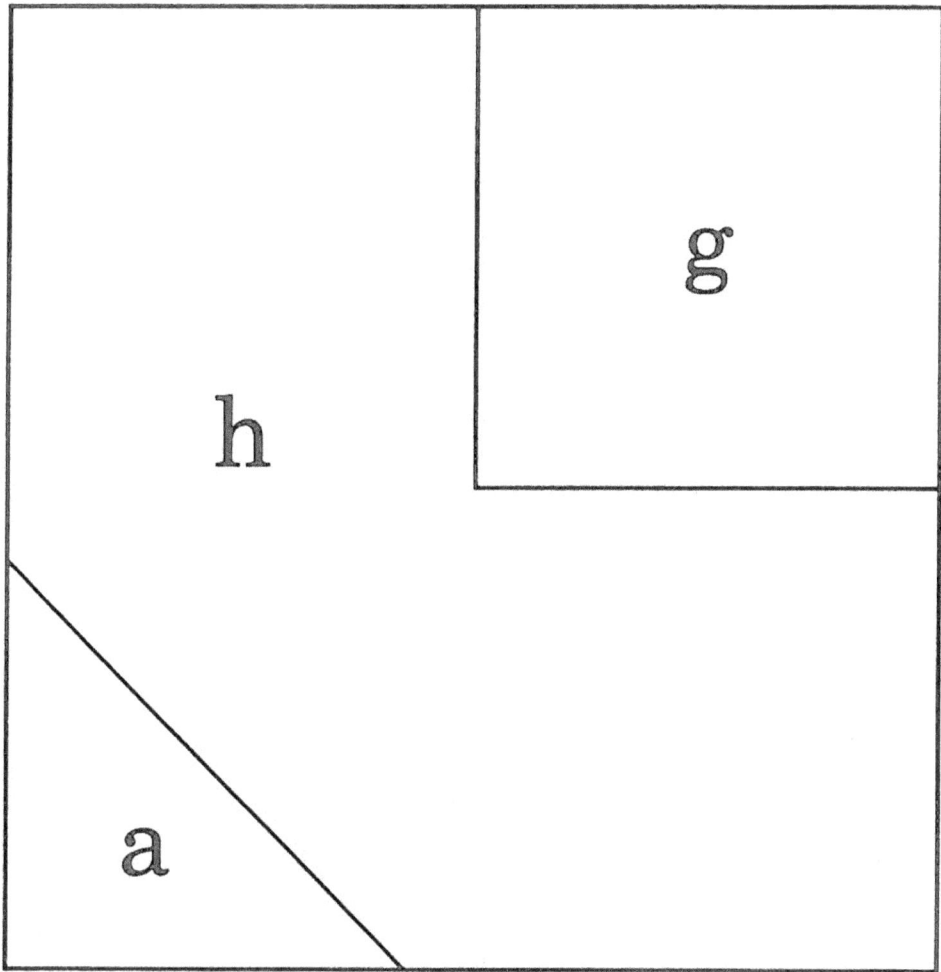

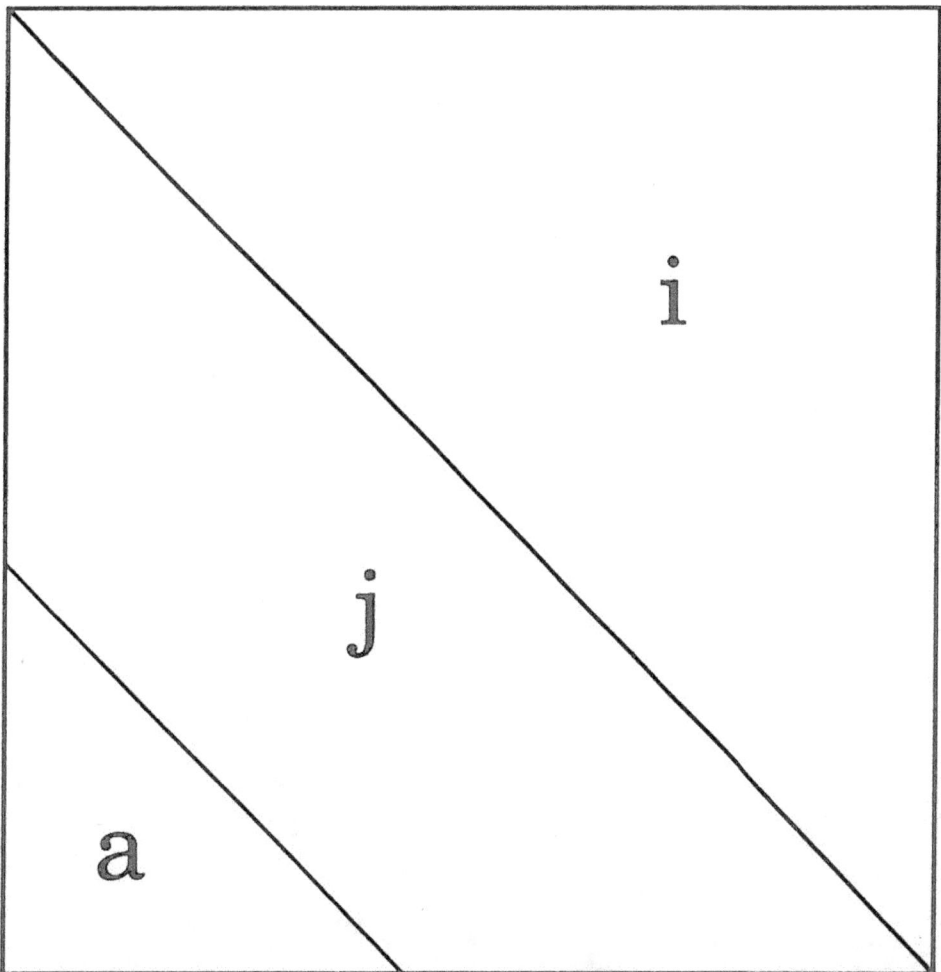

Resource Sheet E-1
TRUE-FALSE QUIZ

1. _____ The session of a church consists of the minister, elders and deacons elected by the congregation.

2. _____ The congregation determines the number of elders and deacons.

3. _____ New elders and deacons are nominated by the session.

4. _____ Persons may be elected to the session or diaconate for a one-year term only.

5. _____ Meetings of the session or diaconate are ordinarily held monthly at a stated time and place.

6. _____ Elders or deacons who fail to attend half of the stated meetings within a year may be removed from office.

7. _____ The minister in charge is the moderator of the session and the chairperson of the diaconate.

8. _____ The session and diaconate must appoint a person to keep an accurate record of proceedings.

9. _____ A majority of the session constitute a quorum unless the congregation has established a different number for a quorum.

10. _____ A person may serve on the session and the diaconate at the same time.

CONSTITUTION REQUIREMENTS
(Organization of Session and Diaconate)

Section 2.42d

The members of the church shall proceed, with the presiding minister in charge, to determine the number of elders to be elected to constitute the session and the type of tenure to which they shall be elected and to elect elders. The ordination and installation of the elders may follow immediately or at a later date. At the option of the members, deacons may be elected, ordained, and installed at this time, at a subsequent congregational meeting, or not at all.

Section 2.53

A congregational meeting of the members of a particular church shall be convened for the following purposes:
a) To determine the type of tenure of office for elders and deacons;
b) To nominate, elect, or accept the resignation of elders and deacons;
c) To establish a quorum of the session or diaconate as less than a majority of the members;
d) To recall an elder or deacon whose service is no longer acceptable to the church.

Section 2.91

In the organization of a particular church, the elders and deacons shall be nominated and elected by the members participating in the organization. In all other cases, it is proper and advisable for the mission to nominate, or to cause to be chosen a committee of the congregation at large to nominate, to the congregation at a meeting called to elect elders and deacons, persons to fill these offices. Other nominations may be made by other members of the church, with the approval of the persons being nominated. The vote may be taken on the nominees at the meeting in which they are presented or at a subsequent congregational meeting. Unless by acclamation, the vote shall be by secret ballot, with a majority of votes cast necessary for election. When there are more nominees than positions to be filled, those receiving the highest number of votes are elected.

Section 2.93

Persons may be elected to the session/diaconate for an indefinite period or for definite terms on a rotation basis. In the organization of a church one type of tenure shall be adopted for the session/diaconate. In an existing church, a change in the type of tenure shall be by actions to dissolve the session/diaconate, install the new type of tenure, and elect members to the session/diaconate according to the new type of tenure. Such actions shall be taken by the congregation in a congregational meeting. If a particular church chooses to elect elders/deacons for a definite term on a rotation basis, the term of office shall be for not less than three years, except when classes are established in the institution of the rotation plan or in cases of unexpired terms.

Section 2.94

If members of the session/diaconate fail to attend half of the stated meetings in a given year without excuse, or if for other non-disciplinary reasons they become unacceptable to the church in the performance of their duties, the session may convene a congregational meeting to consider their removal from office by recall. Before such action is taken, however, opportunity shall be given to the persons involved to address the congregation.

Section 4.1

The session of a particular church consists of the minister in charge and elders elected by the congregation. There must be a minimum of two elders, but the actual number shall be determined by the congregation in accordance with such rules as it may establish.

Section 4.2

In a church which has no pastor, or in the absence of the minister in charge or of the moderator appointed by presbytery, the session may meet and transact any business.

Section 4.3

The session may be convened when two or more of its members so request. The minister in charge may convene the session at any time during or immediately following a regular service of worship and at other times by giving proper notice to session members.

Section 4.4

A majority of the session constitutes a quorum unless the congregation has set a quorum otherwise; but any two elders, in conjunction with the minister may receive members and grant letters of dismission.

ORGANIZATIONAL STRUCTURE: SESSION

Directions: Find the references listed in the *Constitution*. Briefly note on the chart what the *Constitution* states about each item in the left hand column. For each item, describe how your session is organized.

	What the Constitution States	How your session is currently organized
Size of Session	Sections 2.42d; 4.1	
Nomination Process	Sections 2.53b; 2.91	
Tenure	Sections 2.42d; 2.53; 2.93	
Quorum	Sections 2.53c; 4.4	
Session Officers	Sections 3.08; 4.1	
Committees	Section 3.11	
Meetings	Sections 4.2; 4.3	
Attendance	Section 2.94	
Vacancies	Section 2.95	

STANDARD OF PROCEDURE OUTLINE FORM

I. Officers

II. Duties of Officers

III. Nominations and Election of Officers

IV. Terms of Office

V. Vacancies or Absences

VI. Meetings

VII. Attendance

VIII. Quorum

IX. Committees

X. Amendments

ORGANIZATIONAL STRUCTURE: DEACONS

Directions: Find the references listed in the *Constitution*. Briefly note on the chart what the *Constitution* states about each item in the left column. For each item, describe how your diaconate is organized.

	What the Constitution states	How your diaconate is currently organized
Size of Diaconate	Section 2.42d	
Nomination Process	Secton 2.53b; 2.91	
Tenure	Sections 2.53; 2.93	
Quorum	Section 2.53c	
Diaconate Officers		
Committees		
Meetings		
Attendance	Section 2.94	
Vacancies	Section 2.95	

Resource Sheet F-1
SELF-ASSESSMENT INVENTORY

_____ Cumberland Presbyterian Church

NAME _____

ADDRESS _____

PHONE _____ DATE OF BIRTH _____

   Discipleship involves service. Please circle those areas in which you have an interest or skills:

Teaching	Driving
Secretarial work	Tutoring
Building maintenance	Artwork
Youth Advising	Vacation church school
Scout leadership	Hospital visitation
Choir membership	Shut-in errands
Women's circles	Sports programs
Meal preparation	Exercise classes
Meal delivery to shut-ins	Ushering
Committee membership	Mission clothes sorting, delivery
Home-study group membership	Food collection, delivery
Sunday class membership	Church delegate to community organization
New expressions of worship	Greeting at the door on Sundays

Areas not listed, but where I have skills or interests, are:

_____

_____

(Form from *Recruiting and Utilizing The Abilities of Church Leaders,* Continuing Education Series, Unit 6, The Geneva Press, 1975.)

Resource Sheet F-2
A WARNING!
A FABLE OF THE FILE FILLERS

There was once a congregation that was reasonably involved in the work of the church. It had educational programs for children, youth, and adults. Some of its members were studying social and political issues. Others were engaged in projects for improving conditions in the community. The concerns of evangelism, stewardship, and mission were kept before the members. It was not doing all that it could do, nor that it ought to do. Quite a few of its members were not active in any part of its programs. Admittedly, there was room for improvement.

At this point a slick salesman sold them an elaborate filing system, which he represented as just what was needed to solve their problems. Some time later the salesman met one of the church officers and asked, "How are things coming at the church?"

"Oh, fine," was the reply, "that filing system is wonderful. We have complete data on every member and constituent, accurate to the last moment."

"How is the work of the church getting on?"

"Well, it's at a standstill just now. We're using all our leadership to operate the filing system."

(Source: *Recruiting and Utilizing The Abilities of Church Leaders.* Continuing Education Series, Unit 6, The Geneva Press, 1975.)

Situation 1

The youth of the church would like to take a work-trip during the summer to assist in repair of a church building. They need permission from the church session to conduct a fundraising activity.

Situation 2

Members of the CPW have discussed the need for women to be considered as members of the session and diaconate. They are requesting a meeting with each group to discuss their position.

Situation 3

In a meeting of the church session, it has been discussed that the congregation is rather noisy preceding worship. The pastor is asking for suggestons from the session members on how to alleviate the problem.

Situation 4

A church budget proposal has been developed for the coming year. Members of the diaconate are now considering how the financial needs can best be presented to the congregation.

Resource Sheet G-2

NEW MEMBER ENLISTMENT

Listed below are ways used to recruit, prepare and receive members into the church. Circle the number of any method currently being used by your church.

1. A communicant's class for children and youth is conducted each year on the Sundays of the Lenten season.

2. New member orientation sessions for adults are provided on a regular basis.

3. Candidates for membership are received upon profession of faith, reaffirmation of faith or transfer of letter with no other requirements for church membership.

4. The session receives new members during the worship service when the candidates come to the communion table.

5. The session receives members during any meeting of the session.

6. The session meets one Sunday a month for the purpose of receiving new members.

7. Every candidate for membership is expected to study the *Confession of Faith* and meet with the session prior to being received into the church.

8. The pastor visits prospects and invites them to join the church.

9. A team of elders visits prospects and invites them to join the church.

10. Revivals or other evangelistic services are conducted during the year to encourage Christian commitment and church membership.

List below any other methods your church uses for recruiting, preparing and receiving new members into the church:

WHAT SOME CHURCHES ARE DOING ABOUT NEW MEMBERS

1. "Our church has rather severe requirements for membership. We expect every new member to complete our preparatory course of study which meets thirty-six times a year for two years. Candidates for church membership are taken under the care of session until the study units on Bible, doctrine, worship, and churchmanship have been completed. Only then may they ask for examination by the session."

2. "We believe the greatest opportunity for growth in faith occurs after profession of faith is made. Therefore, we examine candidates regarding their motives and sincerity, and commission each new member to a particular area of service as a condition for admission."

3. "Visitors fill in 'Ritual of Fellowship' register. They are sent a letter and assigned to the 'Captain' of the geographic 'parish' in which they live. Someone in the parish visits them. They are invited to 'parish parties' and when they continue coming and/or indicate further interest, or 'desire to join,' the minister visits them. . . . The Membership Committee coordinates the entire program."

4. "Those interested participate in a three-hour Saturday New Member Orientation, and are received by session following this meeting, sometime between the orientation and the next communion. They are given follow-up by sponsors."

5. New members are introduced and honored each month at a fellowship meal.

6. New members are asked to fill out a self-assessment/commitment inventory sheet.

(Quoted items from *Caring For Church Members,* Continuing Education Series, Unit 7, John Knox Press, 1976.)

Resource Sheet G-4

RATING SCALE ON MEMBER CARE

Listed below are some statements about caring for church members. Beneath each statement is a scale with numbers from 1 to 5, covering a range from "very much" to "very little." Read each statement then indicate how you feel it applies to your congregation by circling one of the numbers on the scale beneath it.

1. Church officers make an effort to keep in touch with all church members.

   Very much 1   2   3   4   5 Very little

2. An effort is made to reach each member during the every member canvass.

   Very much 1   2   3   4   5 Very little

3. No systematic effort is made, other than the every member canvass to visit all members.

   Very much 1   2   3   4   5 Very little

4. The pastor follows up on persons who are inactive.

   Very much 1   2   3   4   5 Very little

5. Church officers visit the sick of the congregation when appropriate or call to the attention of the pastor persons who have special need of his/her ministry.

   Very much 1   2   3   4   5 Very little

6. Members of the congregation really support one another in time of need.

   Very much 1   2   3   4   5 Very little

7. Ours is a friendly congregation where visitors and strangers feel welcome.

   Very much 1   2   3   4   5 Very little

Adapted from "Is This True of Us?" p. 21, *Caring For Church Members*, Continuing Education Series, John Knox Press, 1976.

DEFINING THE MISSION OF THE CHURCH

I. *Confession of Faith*
(See sections 5.01-5.09; 5.28-5.31)

Section 5.09—"The church in the world never exists for herself alone, but to glorify God and work for reconciliation through Christ. Christ claims the church and gives her the word and sacraments in order to bring God's grace and judgment to persons."

Section 5.28—"The church, being nurtured and sustained by worship, by proclamation and study of the word, and by the celebration of the sacraments, is commissioned to witness to all persons who have not received Christ as Lord and Savior."

II. *Biblical References*

Isaiah 43:10, 49:6; Matthew 5:14-16, 28:19-20; Luke 24:45-49; John 15:1-11; Acts 1:6-8, 10:39-42; I Peter 2:9.

III. *Theological Understandings*

"The mission of the Cumberland Presbyterian Church is to become God's servant through which the good news of his salvation might be made known to all people. It is the church's mission to extend the ministry of Jesus Christ to the extent that it touches redemptively the lives of all people." (From Report of the Board of Missions, *1978 Minutes of the General Assembly*)

"In this pressing work of preaching the gospel to the unsaved millions at home and abroad, God requires the Cumberland Presbyterian Church to do its full part. We should therefore regard the work of missions not so much a matter of denominational policy as a matter of duty, as the sacred commission and thrust delivered to us by the Master. Everything else is subsidiary and secondary." (From a report by the Committee on Missions to the General Assembly in 1881, taken from *A People Called Cumberland Presbyterian*.)

Resource Sheet H-2

AREAS OF THE CHURCH'S MINISTRY

Worship/Celebration—includes regular services of worship as well as special and seasonal services. Also includes supporting activities such as the choir, preparation for celebrating the sacraments, greeting, ushering, etc.

****

Education—includes activities designed to help people gain knowledge and develop understanding as Christians. Include all regular age group Sunday activities as well as those which may be done at different times of the week or at special times during the year. Also include joint activities with other congregations.

****

Evangelism—includes the activities designed to share your life as a congregation with other people, helping them hear the Good News as we know it through Jesus Christ.

****

Stewardship—includes the activities that focus upon understanding and developing the resources needed for fulfilling the congregation's mission.

Outreach—includes activities which deal with the needs of people in the immediate neighborhood, the larger community, or in other parts of the world. They may be done in cooperation with other congregations.

****

Member Care—includes activities which show people that the congregation cares for them such as visitation, support groups, etc.

****

Buildings and Grounds—includes activities related to the use and maintenance of church buildings, grounds, manse and other special facilities.

****

Fellowship—includes activities which promote friendship and good will among church members and those considering church membership.

****

Leadership and Administration—includes activities which help develop leadership and meetings for planning and implementing programs.

PLANNING GUIDE

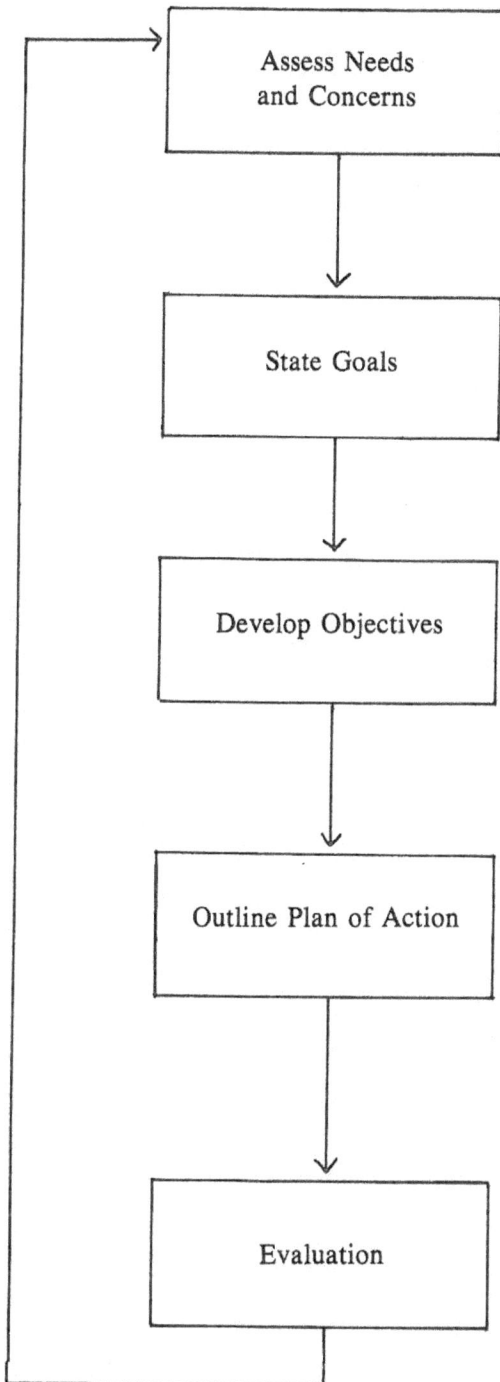

Assess Needs and Concerns	Several needs and concerns have been expressed by the entire group. These should be expanded or refined by small groups to determine goals or desired results related to the needs. *Example:* Financial resources for the church have declined.
State Goals	Goals express the desired results to be achieved through planned activities and programs. *Example:* As members become more aware of their stewardship obligations, financial resources will increase.
Develop Objectives	Objectives indicate specific, measurable steps to reach goals. *Example:* 1) All members will be made aware of budget needs. 2) At least 75% of the budget will be met through pledges.
Outline Plan of Action	The plan indicates the who, what, where and when of implementing the objectives. *Example:* A budget sheet, prepared by the Finance Committee and mailed to every household, will be reviewed and explained at a congregational dinner during November. An every-member canvass will be conducted to encourage members to pledge.
Evaluation	If measurable objectives have been developed, it will be possible to measure results to determine the success of the plan. *Example:* Was the goal achieved? Do the goals and objectives need to be revised? How effective was the plan?

FLOW CHART—CHURCH STRUCTURE

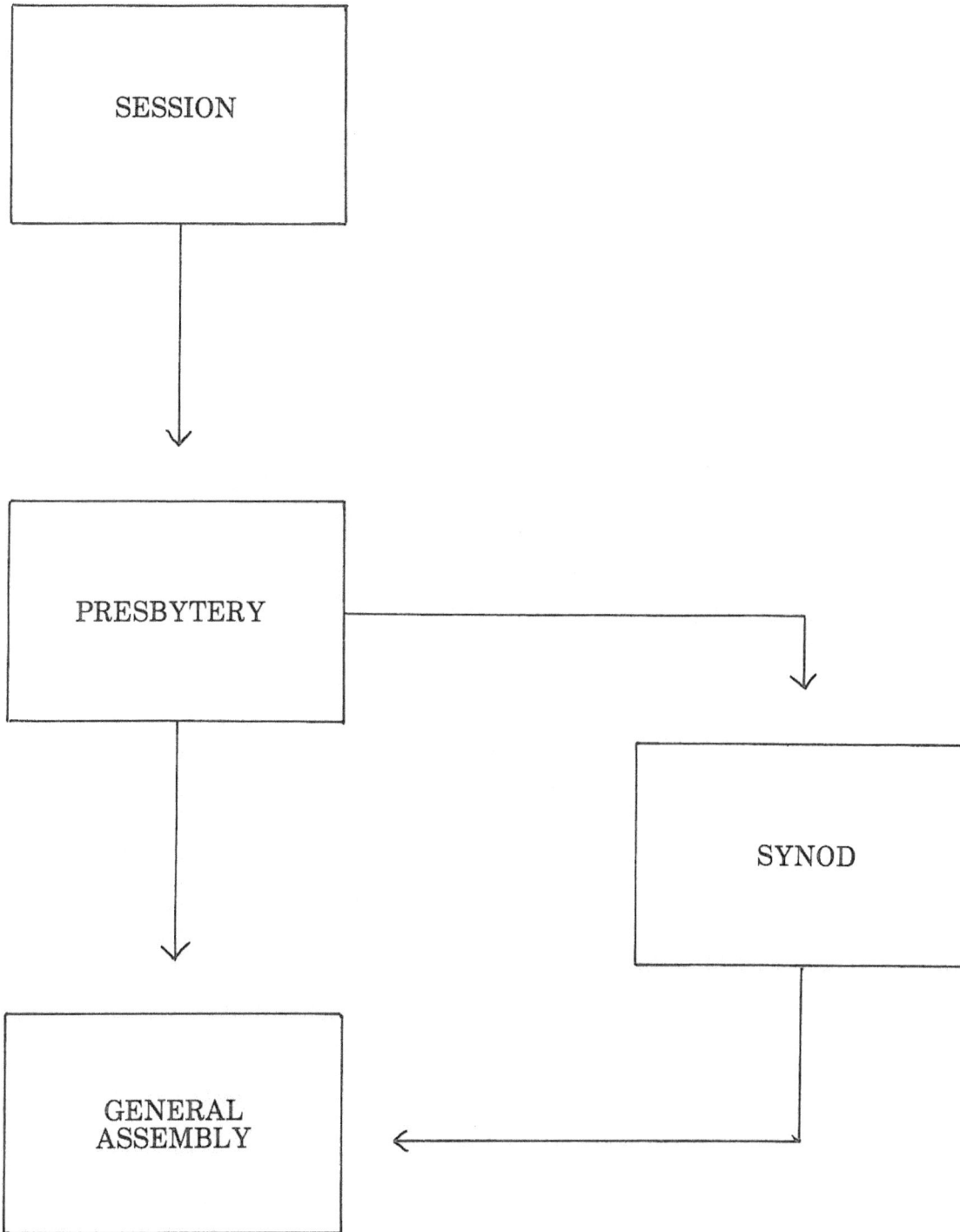

Resource Sheet I-2

FUNCTIONS OF JUDICATORIES

(For a more complete listing see *Constitution,* Sections 4.1-4.7; 5.6-5.7; 8.5-8.6; and 9.4.)

The session has the responsibility to:

—Call a pastor, subject to the approval of presbytery.

—Admonish or suspend members found guilty in a disciplinary hearing, subject to appeal to presbytery.

—Elect representatives to report from higher church judicatories.

—Observe and carry out injunctions of the higher judicatories.

—Submit accurate record of its proceedings to presbytery, at least annually.

The presbytery has the responsibility to:

—Approve ministers to serve as pastors, establish the pastoral relation and dissolve it.

—Review session records and discipline sessions for whatever they may have done contrary to order.

—Examine and decide appeals, protests and referrals brought before it.

—See that the injunctions of the higher judicatories are obeyed.

—Visit particular churches, inquire into their condition and redress the evils that may have arisen in them.

—Settle differences regarding church property and its use.

—Approve location of new churches, relocation of existing churches and proposals and plans of churches considering building or adding to church facilities.

—Unite, divide or dissolve churches; form and receive new churches.

—Take oversight of churches without services of a minister, appointing a minister to moderate the session.

—Formulate budgets and assign shares to churches.

—Elect representatives to higher judicatories.

—Propose measures to the synod or the General Assembly as may be for the good of the church or society in general.

—Submit full and accurate records of proceedings to the synod for review.

The synod has the responsibility to:

—Examine and decide appeals, protests and referrals sent up from presbyteries.

—Review records of presbyteries and redress whatever may have been done contrary to order.

—Organize, divide or dissolve presbyteries.

—Formulate budgets and assign shares to presbyteries.

—Settle differences regarding church property and its use, upon appeal.

—Propose measures to the General Assembly as may be of common advantage to the entire church.

—Submit full and accurate records of proceedings to the General Assembly.

The General Assembly has the responsibility to:

—Receive and decide appeals, protests and referrals brought before it.

—Give counsel concerning the government of the church in all cases submitted.

—Review records of the synods.

—Formulate budgets and assign shares to the presbyteries.

—Promote the prosperity and enlargement of the church; create, divide or dissolve synods.

—Oversee the affairs of the whole church.

Resource sheet I-3

INTERRELATED FUNCTIONS OF JUDICATORIES

Action/Situation   **Judicatories Involved**

1. call a pastor

2. review session records

3. settle local church property dispute

4. form a new church

5. elect General Assembly representatives

6. propose participation of denomination in social
   action events

7. determine synodical boundaries

8. determine presbyterial boundaries

9. establish budget and collect money for
   denominational causes

10. establish and conduct camping programs

11. review presbyterial records

12. settle dispute in session concerning interpreta-
    tion of Constitution

Resource Sheet I-4

SERVING AS REPRESENTATIVES TO HIGHER JUDICATORIES

A delegate to presbytery	A delegate to synod	A commissioner to General Assembly
—is an elder currently serving on the session	—is an elder currently serving on the session	—is an elder currently serving on the session
—is elected as a delegate by the session	—is elected as a delegate by the session	—is elected as a commissioner by the presbytery
—is expected to be present for the duration of the presbytery meeting	—is expected to be present for the duration of the synod meeting	—is expected to be present for the duration of the General Assembly meeting
—is expected to serve on committees as needed	—is expected to serve on committees as needed	—is expected to serve on committees as needed
—may be asked to assist in worship and serving of Holy Communion as needed	—may be asked to assist in worship and serving of Holy Communion as needed	—may be asked to assist in worship and serving of Holy Communion as needed
—is expected to represent the session by voting on issues before the presbytery*	—is expected to represent the session by voting on issues before the synod*	—is expected to represent the presbytery by voting on issues before the General Assembly*
—is expected to report to the session the decisions of the presbytery	—is expected to report to the session the decisions of the synod	—is expected to report to the presbytery the decisions of the General Assembly

*A judicatory after having elected one of its members to represent it at a higher judicatory shall not instruct that member how to vote on the issues; however, counseling representatives is always in order. (Rules of Order, section 11.6)

Resource Sheet I-5
ORGANIZATONAL STRUCTURE OF JUDICATORIES
(Example)

Presbytery

Officers:
  Moderator
  Stated Clerk and Treasurer

Staff:
  Executive/Coordinator

Committees/Boards/Agencies:
  Missions (CPW)
  Finance
  Christian Education
  Ministry
  Christian Social Relations
  Inter-Church Relations

Synod

Officers:
  Moderator
  Stated Clerk and Treasurer

Staff:
  Executive/Coordinator
  Executive Committee

Committees/Boards/Agencies:
  Missions (CPW)
  Finance
  Christian Education
  Christian Social Relations

General Assembly
Cumberland Presbyterian Churches

Officers:
  Moderator
  Assistant Moderator
  Stated Clerk and Treasurer
  Assistant Stated Clerk

Executive Committee:
  Moderator
  Past Moderator
  Seven Members at large

Boards:
  Trustees of Bethel College
  Trustees of Memphis Theological
    Seminary
  Finance
  Christian Education
  Trustees of Children's Home
  Missions
  Trustees of Historical Foundation

Commissions:
  Chaplains
  Christian Social Relations
  On the Ministry

Committees:
  Inter-Church Relations
  Joint Committee on Unification
  Judiciary
  Theological Studies
  Place of Meeting

For a listing of personnel see current copies of presbytery and synod minutes and *General Assembly Yearbook.*

Resource Sheet J-1

DEALING WITH CONFLICT

A. Why Deal With Conflict At All?

"The church is one body with many different parts working interdependently. To ignore, suppress, or hide conflict among the members, or to deal with it arbitrarily or in a way that excludes those who may be involved, means that the church either functions poorly or that some parts don't function at all. Our own bodies are made up of different, interdependent parts; when one part gets stiff or sore, we find out what's wrong with it and do something about it so that we can function well again. Just as we have to tell the physician which part hurts and how long the pain has been going on before a remedy can be found, so we have to SAY what makes us uneasy or angry to be able to work in the church toward "diagnosis and cure." The alternative to finding creative ways to deal openly with conflict is to risk the undermining of the mission of the church at the least, and at worst, to allow unexpressed conflict to grow until it erupts in a sudden, destructive action, dividing the church body."

B. How Do We Handle Conflict?

"Conflict can generally be dealt with in two ways: *competitively,* where one individual or group has to lose the "battle" and the other wins; or *integratively,* where individuals are encouraged to express all differing values and opinions and to resolve any conflict through a mutual process. When conflict resolution is competitive, groups usually are pulled farther apart and the reconciling ministry to which we are called becomes almost impossible. Integrating conflict requires a time and a place for open expression and a method for discovering common goals that may result in new mutual values arising out of the original differences."

C. Basic Principles for Resolving Conflict

1. Deal openly with conflict as soon as possible. Attempts to suppress a problem may only lead to extreme and destructive action.
2. Try to resolve conflict through a mutual, integrative process, giving all individuals involved an opportunity to express ideas and opinions.
3. It is sometimes helpful to have a trained professional "third party" to act in the role of mediator.
5. Pay attention to physical factors which can aid in a meeting to resolve conflict, such as direct eye contact with the person you are talking or listening to, meeting on neutral ground, meeting when persons involved are able to think and reason clearly (avoid late night meetings when persons are tired), and meeting in a room that is arranged comfortably for all involved.
6. Avoid letting situations become "shouting matches" where verbal (or physical) attacks are made on different parties involved.
7. Consider following a five step process for conflict resolution:
    a. Formulate a statement of the problem.
    b. Clarify the dimensions of the conflict.
    c. Brainstorm all possible solutions to the conflict.
    d. Identify the consequences of alternative solutions.
    e. Choose a mutually acceptable solution.

(Taken from *Dealing Creatively With Conflict,)* Unit 3, Continuing Education Series, The Geneva Press, 1975.)

(For additional suggestions see Chapter V-VII in *Leadership and Conflict,* Creative Leadership Series, Speed B. Leas, Abingdon Press, Nashville, 1982)